T0246608

HOW TO DELIVER

BAD NEWS

AND

GET AWAY WITH IT

— A MANAGER'S GUIDE —

MAHESH GURUSWAMY

GREENLEAF
BOOK GROUP PRESS

Published by Greenleaf Book Group Press
Austin, Texas
www.gbgpress.com

Distributed by Greenleaf Book Group

For ordering information or special discounts for bulk purchases,
please contact Greenleaf Book Group at PO Box 91869, Austin,
TX 78709, 512.891.6100.

Design and composition by Greenleaf Book Group
Cover design by Greenleaf Book Group

Publisher's Cataloging-in-Publication data is available.

Print ISBN: 979-8-88645-269-3

eBook ISBN: 979-8-88645-270-9

To offset the number of trees consumed in the printing of our
books, Greenleaf donates a portion of the proceeds from each
printing to the Arbor Day Foundation. Greenleaf Book Group
has replaced over 50,000 trees since 2007.

Printed in the United States of America on acid-free paper

25 26 27 28 29 30 31   10 9 8 7 6 5 4 3 2 1

First Edition

To my wife, Krishma, and son, Vivaan. Their relentless optimism, support, and unconditional love helped me write this book. And to all my supporters on LinkedIn and Substack who encouraged me to write this.

CONTENTS

FOREWORD

A s someone who has known Mahesh Guruswamy for a few years and mentored him in his early days as a chief technology officer, I'm honored to introduce his insightful work to readers.

In the ever-evolving landscape of modern business, delivering bad news is an inevitable challenge every manager must face. Whether it's addressing performance issues, navigating project delays, or handling dissatisfied customers, effectively communicating difficult information is a critical skill for any leader. Mahesh's book is an essential guide for managers looking to master this complex art.

Drawing from his extensive experience as a seasoned product development executive and CTO, Mahesh offers a wealth of practical advice and strategies for delivering bad news with empathy, clarity, and professionalism. He delves into the nuances of tailoring your message to different audiences, from team members and stakeholders to customers and executives. Through relatable anecdotes and real-world examples, Mahesh illustrates how to navigate these challenging conversations while maintaining trust and minimizing fallout.

One of the key strengths of this book is Mahesh's emphasis on emotional intelligence and the human element of management. He reminds us that behind every difficult conversation is a person with their own unique perspectives, fears, and motivations. By approaching these interactions with empathy and a genuine desire to understand, managers can foster a culture of open communication and collaboration, even in the face of adversity.

Moreover, Mahesh doesn't shy away from the tough topics. He tackles the delicate nature of delivering performance improvement plans, the art of disagreeing with grace, and the importance of being receptive to feedback as a leader. His insights are grounded in a deep understanding of organizational dynamics and the realities of the modern workplace.

Throughout the book, Mahesh's engaging writing style and relatable storytelling make complex concepts accessible and actionable. Whether you're a seasoned executive or a first-time manager, you'll find valuable takeaways and practical tips you can implement immediately in your leadership practice.

In a world where the ability to communicate effectively can make or break a career, *How to Deliver Bad News and Get Away with It* is a must-read for anyone looking to become a more confident, empathetic, and effective leader. I highly recommend this book to anyone seeking to enhance their leadership skills and build stronger, more resilient teams. Mahesh's insights will help you deliver bad news more effectively and foster a culture of trust, transparency, and growth within your organization.

—SANJAY TIWARY

Chief technology officer at Spectrum Equity and former
chief technology officer at Audible, Grubhub, and Bankrate

INTRODUCTION

O ver the years, I have read many management and leadership books. Largely, they fall into two categories. The first category covers the broad strokes of how to lead and manage teams. Good examples are *The Effective Executive* by Peter Drucker, *Leadership on the Line* by Ronald Heifetz and Marty Linsky, and *How to Win Friends and Influence People* by Dale Carnegie, among others. These books cover a lot of wide-ranging topics but never go into much depth for any one specific area. They give the reader a general sense of what it takes to succeed as a leader and a manager. The second category of books covers the glorious beginning—how to set the stage and set your team up for success. Essentially, they focus on topics such as how to hire people, build rapport with your team, set goals and track them, and so on. Great examples are *Turn the Ship Around!* by L. David Marquet; *Leadership Is Language*, also by L. David Marquet; and *Drive* by Daniel Pink. There are very few books that cover the messy middle. *How to Deliver Bad News* is about the messy middle.

After spending more than two decades in the technology industry, a decade as a people manager, and the last five years as an executive, I can say with certainty that many managers will spend most of their time in the messy middle. For example, this is what my calendar looks like for the next five days: I have two status meetings, and I'll have to deliver bad news to the stakeholders in one of them. I have four one-on-one meetings. Two of them are with individuals who are having performance issues. One of these individuals is a manager who is having a conflict with his peer and wants me to resolve it. My last meeting is with my manager, who is upset at me for not hitting one of my goals. This is not a one-off week for me. Most of my weeks are like this. And I am not alone. Most of my successful peers and managers have weekly schedules that look like mine. For a while, I would often ask my bosses and peers how they learned the skill of delivering bad news. Almost always, their answer was, "You will learn it over time," "There is no compression algorithm for experience," or some variation of needing to put in the time. Experience is one of the best teachers, but managers don't have to navigate the messy middle without help. That is why I wrote this book.

The book covers three broad areas. The first is all about detection and preparation. Detection is about how to spot problematic situations that might require you to intervene and deliver bad news, such as an employee who is not pulling their weight, runaway projects, and so on. Preparation is tailoring the tone and temperature of your bad news to match the situation. For example, your response to an employee slipping on their commitments for the first time must be softer than it is for the third time. The second area the book covers is tailoring the bad news to different parties. We first discuss effective writing in general and then move on to addressing different groups, such as stakeholders, your team, individuals on your team, your boss, and so on. The third area the book covers is how to react when you (gasp!) become the unfortunate recipient of bad news. This book's stories and examples will be very familiar to managers of software development teams, but the situations and their lessons apply to any people leader whose job is to deliver value to their company through their team.

One word of caution: a lot of this book's content is the messy stuff that managers deal with daily, so please don't let this book deter you from pursuing a career in management. People management is an extremely rewarding career choice if you walk into it with the right mindset.

Let's get going, then, shall we?

CHAPTER 1

How to Determine It's Time to Deliver Bad News

Over the last two decades, the realities of what a manager is and does have dramatically changed. Long gone are the days of type A, loud, cigar-smoking, suit-wearing men giving orders to perpetually overworked and scared employees. They have been replaced with diverse leaders who encourage bottom-up thinking and use empathy and empowerment to motivate employees. However, in this loud drumbeat we hear everywhere of how to behave like an all-empathetic, all-empowering, all-caring twenty-first-century manager, an important fact gets lost.

The hard truth is, at the end of the day, you as a manager are responsible for making sure you are getting the most out of your team and delivering a positive return on investment for the company you work for. You are automatically underwriting all the decisions your team is making. If you constantly keep underwriting bad decisions, at some point your boss will fire you. I am sure we managers have had moments when we think, "I am not sure my team is doing the right thing here. Should I intervene or should I let them figure this out?" This chapter is about how to detect situations that might require you to deliver bad news later. Those situations generally revolve around people or projects.

People Issues

Employees and their work-related issues are one of the most difficult categories of issues to fix and the bane of every manager's existence. They can cause a lot of damage if left unchecked. There are two broad categories of people-related issues in which a manager needs to intervene: individual performance issues and personnel conflicts.

Chapter 4 is entirely dedicated to dealing with performance issues, so I don't go into much detail here. The long and short is, if anyone (somebody on your team or someone in the company) comes to you with concerns about an employee's performance or you have your own suspicions, please act on it. It is always easy to ignore these things, but listen to the annoying voice in your head. Let's get into personnel conflicts and how to resolve them.

Personnel conflicts can severely affect the productivity of teams. Conflicts typically happen when two people (or groups of people) have to align on a path forward and are unable to do so. In my career I have spent thousands of hours trying to resolve conflicts inside and outside my team, and I have come to the conclusion that convincing people to do something they don't want to do is a fool's errand. I have tried cajoling and using authority, their bosses' authority, hardball tactics, softball tactics, and a million other things. I even read Harvard's MBA course material on negotiation and tried applying them! I can't point to any of those things as a sure shot way of resolving conflicts.

Experience has shown me that the most effective mechanism to resolve conflicts is to create a set of employee behavioral tenets (a.k.a. values) that clearly describes how employees should resolve conflicts on their own. This way you are not trying to change people's behaviors every time there is a conflict but are preemptively setting the expectations for acceptable behavior and outcomes, ideally even before they are hired. Your company values should include values that tell employees how to navigate conflict situations. Amazon has "Disagree and Commit" and "Earn Trust," which help employees navigate conflicts and, in my opinion, are the best example of how company values can be used to resolve conflicts.[1] Netflix also has a handful of values that tell their employees how to navigate conflicts, such as, "You use data to inform your intuition and choices," "You make decisions mostly based on their long term, rather than near term, impact," "You debate ideas openly, and help implement whatever decision is made even when you disagree," "You make tough decisions without agonizing or long delay," and so on.[2]

---

1 Amazon Jobs, "Leadership Principles," accessed March 11, 2024, https://www.amazon.jobs/content/en/our-workplace/leadership-principles.

2 Netflix Jobs, "Netflix Culture—Seeking Excellence," accessed March 31, 2024, https://jobs.netflix.com/culture.

Google, on the other hand, does not have a company value around conflict. I have many friends and family who work at Google and can say with some level of certainty that Google struggles to make decisions as a company. There is a lot of discussion and heated debate about even the simplest decisions that slow progress down to a crawl. Google is not the only one with this glaring deficit. Microsoft is another one, and we all have heard about the horrors of politics that employees have to deal with over there. In fact, I would guess that most companies do not have explicitly defined company values that provide their employees with a blueprint for navigating conflicts without breaking trust with each other.

After encountering multiple companies that didn't have corporate values around conflict management, I decided to create my own set of tenets that I hand out to my team. This is what I use:

- Never shy away from conflicts. Yes, it will be uncomfortable, but as a leader, you are obligated to lean in and find a path forward.

- Display a high level of emotional intelligence. Never become passive-aggressive or aggressive.

- Have a cause and conviction.

- Base your arguments on sound business judgment, not your personal opinion.

- Validate your assumptions with your peers, your manager, other teams, and against industry standards.

- There are no absolutes in life or business; be ready to compromise.

Feel free to repurpose these tenets for your team as you see fit. The bottom line is, focus on creating a conflict resolution blueprint for your team versus focusing on getting better at teaching individuals how to resolve every single conflict.

Project Management Issues

The second category, project management, is the crucible where every manager's dreams and aspirations will be crushed, melted, and reforged into the realities of the revered quarterly time frames in the corporate world. Okay, that is being a bit too dramatic, but project management is another area where managers need to intervene if they see issues crop up. Project management issues typically fall into two buckets—issues that crop up during planning and issues that show up during execution. Both of these buckets can involve communication issues as well. Let's unpack.

Planning Issues

The biggest planning-related complications occur when the team is planning large projects that could span multiple months. I can almost guarantee that if you ask your team for an end-to-end estimate for full delivery of any project that will go beyond two or three months, they will tell you the answer is six months. The key is to ask the team to break the project down into milestones and ensure that the distance between each milestone is less than one month. If the team is unable to scope the milestone down, then start cutting scope until you get a milestone that is reasonably timed. This is when you can also find out if your team is sandbagging estimates and/or making incorrect assumptions. If you don't do this exercise, I can almost guarantee failure. The most a team can plan for accurately is about a month. Anything beyond that, I can almost guarantee some gremlin (scope creep, bugs, acts of god, vacations, etc.) sideswiping the project, which will push it off the tracks. So, to recap, if your team can't scope down projects to, at the most, one-month customer-facing milestones, you as their manager have to intervene and work with your team to scope it down to under a month. If your team is absolutely unable to figure this out after a lot of hand-holding, you probably have the wrong people on your team. I understand that most teams are not filled with rock star employees, but there should be at least one senior-level employee on the team who can help you get the team to do what they don't want to do.

Execution Issues

Execution issues typically center on timelines slipping because of three reasons:

1. Inertia setting in because the team can't agree on a path forward—a.k.a. analysis paralysis

2. Timelines slipping because the team keeps uncovering new complexities

3. Individuals on the team having a performance issue

I do not talk about the third point here because I cover it in a later chapter. My rule of thumb is, if an individual misses a deadline three times in a row with scope and timelines remaining relatively constant, then something is going on with that individual. Let's unpack the others.

Analysis Paralysis

If you put a smart group of people in a room and ask them to solve a complex problem, there is about an 80 percent chance they are going to get deadlocked on a path forward. This problem is especially acute when they are working on a blue-sky initiative with high-risk and high-reward transformative concepts. The biggest delays usually occur during the planning/design phase of the project. Greenfield initiatives—new projects from scratch—are a magnet for a thousand great design ideas and a thousand more bad ideas. The more people involved in the project, the worse it becomes.

When I am kicking off greenfield projects, I always make sure there is *one* person responsible for making all the critical high-level decisions in the project. I typically assign a senior employee (a senior engineer, senior product manager, etc.) responsible for design, and I empower them to make critical design decisions for the project. This doesn't mean they operate in a vacuum. Peer feedback is essential, but I empower the leader to move forward with design choices even if it isn't super popular with their peers, as long as I (the manager) am comfortable enough to underwrite that decision. It is natural for humans to look for consensus, and this is where delays come in. Smart folks will pore over every single negative feedback and try to figure out how to accommodate that feedback into their design.

One of the mechanisms I use to enforce efficient decision-making is design milestones. I don't give teams more than a month to hash out the design for any project. Most designs should typically take a couple of weeks. If I notice the team missing the "design locked" deadlines a few times in a row, then I intervene. I typically sit down with the project lead and prioritize the outstanding design decisions based on what we believe is needed for the first version of the product. We then talk about how much additional time it will add to the overall project and start ruthlessly culling that list. As long as the decision is a two-way door (expanded further in Chapter 13), which most decisions are, I am comfortable pushing forward and moving the middle and lower priority changes to later phases.

Timelines Slipping

This is also a common occurrence in complex projects. The team starts micro-slipping on their planned projects, which accumulates into full-blown project delays. I typically intervene when the team misses deadlines on a project more than twice on the same tasks.

Driven employees are always looking to make their mark on the team and the company by going the extra mile, so when the scope of the project changes, they just try to absorb it in their current timelines by working a bit harder. Obviously, the team can't absorb this forever and at some point delays creep into the project. The fix is straightforward. Take a pause and sit down with the project lead to either cull the new scope or, if the new scope is absolutely needed, replan and adjust timelines as needed.

However, if this happens a handful of times, you have to take a stronger stance and start questioning the entire project and push the team to figure out the bare minimum feature set that's needed to get a delightful product to the customers sooner rather than later. Feature scope creep is not the only flavor you will encounter. Additional complexity can easily creep into large complex projects. However, the solution is the same. Pause, figure out if the scope is needed, replan, and readjust timelines.

Communication Issues

There is nothing like a game of badly played telephone to ruin project timelines, destroy trust, and crater promotions. The biggest communication issues occur when communicating statuses upward and sideways. Imagine for a second you were out sick on status update day. You wake up bleary eyed and shoot off a hastily written email to your team saying you are sick and asking one of your sharpest employees to go represent the team in the weekly status meeting. When it is your team's turn to report on status, this is what your employee says: "Hmm, it feels like we are still green, but it is hard to say with certainty if it will stay green next week. There are still a few weeks' worth of work remaining."

The project sponsor, now a bit worried, asks, "This is the first I am hearing about this. Why do you think you won't be green?"

"I don't know."

"Then how do you know you won't be green next week?"

"I don't, but we haven't planned the last two weeks of work, so there *could* be unknowns there."

"Can you take a rough guess on where the risks might be?"

"I don't think there are many risks."

"You just said there might be risks."

"Actually, I said 'unknowns,' not 'risks.' I don't know if one of those unknowns will become a risk."

Sigh.

A week later. "Did you hear that MG's project is delayed by multiple months?"

"Where did you hear this?"

"Oh, Andy told me."

"I just had a one-on-one with MG an hour ago, and he told me things were on track."

"Oh, I don't know. I am just telling you what Andy told me."

"I think I will bring it up with my boss just in case."

This is obviously a hyperbolic example. The point I am trying to make is, managers typically have more context about the state of things than the individuals on the project, so you have to keep an eye out for incorrect messaging about your team and intervene as soon as possible, especially for status updates. I keep in close touch with all my stakeholders, and I tightly control what statuses are communicated upward and sideways. If I fall sick on status day, I write up the status and send it to all my stakeholders, including the person who ends up representing the team on my behalf. Nothing against engineers, but I have found that product managers are often better suited for reporting statuses (especially a bad one) than the engineers on the team. So, whenever I am out of pocket, I typically lean on my product counterpart to represent the team in status meetings, metrics reviews, and so on. Engineers are way too truthful.

A QUICK RECAP

1. Bottom-up doesn't work all the time. There will be situations where you have to lean in, take charge, intervene, and forcibly change things.

2. Create tenets that employees can use to resolve conflicts on their own versus solving it for them.

3. Force your team to break down larger projects into smaller customer-facing milestones that are less than two months apart.

4. Create time boundaries for the design phase of projects and intervene if the team misses the deadlines more than a couple of times. Pay very close attention to this milestone for greenfield projects. Be comfortable making two-way-door decisions.

5. Watch out for scope creep.

6. Keep an ear out for incorrect narratives about your team or the projects they are working on and intervene quickly. Be *very* careful of delegating communications to someone on your team.

CHAPTER 2

How to Prepare
to Deliver Bad News

I t is common knowledge that one of the main skills that managers need to build is the ability to communicate effectively with different audiences. There is a lot of literature available (online and in books) that gets into how to tailor your communication style to different audiences. However, one thing books leave out is how to tailor the tone and temperature of your communication based on the situation. Pressure, conflict, or disagreement situations require a different tone of voice compared to peaceful situations. There might be times when you want to get your frustration across to the other person (or group) clearly, but other times you might not want to just yet. This chapter is about how to deliver the bad news at different temperatures.

But before we get into that, let's talk about the "why." Shouldn't we all just speak our minds? Isn't it best to simply express your disagreement directly? Aren't we required to bring our authentic self to work? Isn't it prudent to not beat around the bush? Shouldn't we practice radical candor?

I have been managing people for more than a decade. I have been keenly observing people even longer than that. I am not stretching the truth when I say that most of my modest success in management is directly related to being able to predict how individuals or teams will behave in war and peaceful situations. I have seen up close how poorly people behave in moments of conflict or disagreement. I now firmly believe that most of the people in the workforce are not equipped to handle disagreements or conflict situations, especially if they end up on the losing side.

The stronger and longer the disagreement, the deeper the resentment in the hearts of the people who are in it, even if the outcome is a compromise that benefits both parties. Most people will remember the pain and the emotional toll of the conflict rather than the relief of the outcome. They will personalize the conflict. They will remember names and times.

In my career, I have always taken the approach of raising the temperature slowly, and I wholeheartedly recommend that approach to all the readers who want to deliver bad news. There have been exceptions to this when I have raised the temperature in the very first conversation, but they are exceptions and not the norm. When I raise the temperature slowly, it does a few things. First, it doesn't put people on their heels, and hence they are more open to sharing what they are actually feeling. Second, they will be more open to compromises, and last, they won't hate me if they end up losing their argument. I know lots of famous technology companies say that they don't do things for the sake of social cohesion. Said another way, they don't care if employees piss each other off as long as the business keeps moving forward. I think that is a dangerous stance to take. I can't imagine working in a team where there is zero social cohesion. If your employees can't stand each other, you don't have a team anymore; you just have a bunch of mercenaries who will stab each other in the back when given a chance.

So what does raising the temperature slowly mean? In practice, it means you start off by presenting an alternative hypothesis (after fully understanding the option on the table) instead of downright dismissing the one presented by the other person (or team) and taking care not to elicit a strong emotional reaction.

Here is a real example. When I disagree with a design decision my team is making, this is what my low-temperature pushback will sound like:

> I am *not sure* this is the right way to go about it. I have seen evidence from [insert relevant career anecdote] that this won't work. Have we considered solving this by doing [insert your option]?

The emphasized words are what makes this work. You are starting the conversation by not outright shooting the other person's idea down. This gentle pushback will invite a healthy, thoughtful, and objective debate as opposed to an unhealthy emotional response. In general, stay away from any absolutist statements. Those will almost always elicit a strong emotional response as opposed to robust discussion and debate.

However, there are situations when you have to increase the temperature. The only situations I can think of where raising the temperature is warranted are one-way doors or people problems. I go into one-way-door decisions versus two-way-door decisions in a later chapter. To put it simply, two-way-door decisions are dramatically cheaper to unwind than one-way-door decisions. Let's look at one-way doors first.

If you believe (with rock-solid data to back up that assertion) that unwinding the decision will be prohibitively expensive, managers are obligated to increase the temperature eventually. Start with low-temperature pushback and see if you can get your team to see your side of the equation. If it doesn't work, increase the temperature.

Here is an example of high-temperature pushback for the same situation we previously discussed:

> This is a bad idea, and *I disagree* with this decision. I have seen evidence from [insert relevant career anecdote] that this won't work. It will affect our company by [some catastrophic outcome]. We should do [insert your option] instead.

Just saying the words "I disagree" will elicit a strong emotional reaction from the other person. I know it is fashionable to use "Disagree and Commit" as a conflict resolution technique, but in practice, it is very hard for people to disagree and commit without taking an emotional hit, especially if they had put in a lot of work to make their case. But in this scenario, it is warranted because the team is about to make a one-way-door decision that you disagree with and your previous attempts of nudging the team in the right direction didn't work.

The other situation where you might want to raise the temperature is when giving critical feedback to your team. Let's look at this example.

The work quality of one of the individuals on your team is slipping. Low-temperature feedback will look something like this:

Hey, I have started noticing that your work quality has been slipping. I noticed [insert specific examples] where you were consistently late. Do you have any thoughts on what caused the delays? What can I help with?

Low-temperature critical feedback will empower the other person to open lines of communication, and in the previous example the person receiving the feedback will feel comfortable sharing what's on their mind because of the tone of the feedback. One never knows what people are going through in their personal lives. Starting with low-temperature feedback will allow you to help the other person as opposed to putting them on the defensive.

However, if the same individual's performance doesn't become better after repeated nudges, you will have to raise the temperature. High-temperature feedback with the same individual will be something like this:

Bob, your work has been slipping consistently. That is unacceptable and has to be rectified immediately. What do we need to do to get you there?

The word "unacceptable" raises the temperature, and if the person still doesn't get the message, you probably have to start creating a performance improvement plan for this employee, which is covered in Chapter 4.

Table 1. A message at different temperatures

Low temperature	High temperature	Rude
I don't think this is the right way to do it.	This is a bad idea.	This is stupid.
You made people uncomfortable in that meeting.	You were rude and condescending.	You were a jerk.
I am not sure that is what customers want.	Customers will not use it.	There is no way customers would want anything to do with it.
Sorry, I don't understand your line of reasoning; can you explain your rationale again, or maybe in a different way?	What you are saying doesn't make much sense.	What you are suggesting is nonsense.

Table 1 shows some more examples of how the same message will sound at different temperatures. And yes, I wouldn't recommend using rudeness to get your point across, and yes, don't be rude even if you are right and the other person is wrong. If you ever go that far, you have to apologize to the other person.

The bottom line is, if you want to build trust with your team and create an environment of two-way communication, you absolutely have to know how to deliver the same message at different temperatures.

A QUICK RECAP

1. Learn how to slowly ramp up the temperature in conflict situations.

2. Low-temperature messages will encourage dialogue.

3. High-temperature messages will elicit a strong emotional reaction, *but* they will get your point across.

4. There is a fine line between a high-temperature message and rudeness. Don't cross it.

CHAPTER 3

How to Deliver Bad (and Good!) News in Writing

A long time ago, in a parallel universe, I was a first-time CTO. Okay, fine, I lied; it was this universe, but being a first-time CTO sure did feel like being in a parallel universe. I had a lot of big ideas. I was determined to break a bunch of eggs and make a glorious splash in my first ninety days. After spending a month talking to everybody on my team, I made a list of some things I wanted to change. The first change I wanted to make was in the leadership team that directly reported to me. It wasn't so much a change as it was a realignment of leadership values that I wanted them to uphold. Specifically, I wanted my direct reports to use the same leadership values I used when it came to making business decisions. Just for the sake of completeness, here are the values I use as a leader:

1. Leaders empower their teams to make decisions versus making it themselves.

2. Leaders don't shy away from hard problems.

3. Leaders are emotionally intelligent.

4. Leaders are T-shaped; they have depth in one or multiple areas, but they don't hesitate to jump into unknown areas.

5. Leaders are comfortable with ambiguity.

6. Leaders act like owners. Nothing is beneath them.

7. Leaders have a very flexible growth-oriented mindset. They believe that when presented with a seemingly insurmountable task, all they need to do is learn new skills that will allow them to complete that task.

8. Leaders never shy away from conflicts.

9. Leaders understand the mechanics of how the company makes money.

10. Leaders recruit and retain the best.

I wanted my leadership team to embrace the values that I believed in. So I wrote a quick email to my leadership team with a couple of lines about realigning the team to start using the new set of values and listed out the values themselves. I followed that up with a live Zoom meeting, in which I was determined to make a soaring speech that would end with tears and applause.

I jumped on the call with my team, and I jumped into a monologue about how I came up with the values, why they were important, and how I wanted the leadership team to embrace the new values. After I ended my spiel, I waited for the applause, but

I only received blank stares. About twenty seconds of uncomfortable silence passed before one of the directors piped up and reluctantly asked me, "So . . . what do you want us to do?" I knew right then that I had stepped on a rake. I tried to salvage that conversation by launching into another meaningless monologue but was thankfully saved by the bell. We ran out of time.

I had recorded that meeting, so I watched the recording that night. It was terrible. I was terrible. I don't have a very loud or deep voice. I probably sound okay in a face-to-face conversation, but on video (as I discovered that night), I sounded like I was whispering. I sounded like an insecure ghoul trying to scare humans for the first time and failing. I was speaking incomplete sentences. My enunciation consistently lost steam toward the end of most of my sentences. My monologue was filled with pointless filler words like "so," "like," "yeah," and so on. Even if I ignored all of that and just looked at whether I clearly conveyed what I wanted to, it was clear that I didn't. I didn't explain the "why." Why do I want the leadership team to adopt a new set of values? Why do I think these new values will help? How do we enforce these new values? Are these values just for leaders, or should they be pushed down to the teams as well?

I spent the next few days writing a document that explained the "why" in detail. I added narratives to each value and explained them in detail. I went into how I came up with the value, why the value was important, how to use it daily, and what positive changes leaders could expect once they embraced the new value. Once I was done, I sent the document over for a preread to my leadership team and then pulled them all together for a discussion about the new values rather than a speech. I watched the recording of that meeting as well that night, and I wasn't embarrassed at all.

By the way, if you want a ready-made set of leadership values to use with your teams, feel free to repurpose what I outlined earlier.

Verbal versus Written Communication

If you look at any job description for managers, invariably you will see "excellent communication skills" as a required skill in it. Sometimes it will say "excellent written and verbal skills," other times it will say "experience communicating to executives," or it will say "experience communicating to technical and non-technical audiences alike," and so on. My guess is most people don't give too much thought to that requirement when hunting or applying for managerial roles. I would bet a dollar that most people look at that skill requirement and think, "At least I have that skill nailed down." I mean, we have been learning (and practicing) how to read and write since we were five, have we not? The way I see it, a lot of managers and leaders out there are absolutely terrible at communicating. They are terrible not because they don't know the mechanics of how to put words together in the right sequences when they write emails or when they are talking to their team. It is because they misunderstand what "excellent communication skills" means. I am going to stray a bit from the themes of the previous chapters and include some good news along with the bad, just to show I am not a complete downer. This chapter naturally builds on knowing how to use the warm or cool temperatures of the previous chapter and the discussions of knowing your audience from Chapter 1, since audience is the most important factor in crafting effective written communication.

Excellent communication skills in the context of managers mean something deeper. It is not so much about whether your audience understands the words, but about understanding the emotion behind those words. How do you want the audience to feel after they read your email? How do you want your team to feel after you talk to them? How do you want your stakeholders to feel after you deliver the status to them? Expressing the appropriate emotion for the situation is what effective communication is all about. Don't get me wrong; grammatically correct sentences do matter, but the emotional strength of the words matters more than the order you write them in.

So how do you effectively communicate emotions? Most people assume that the spoken word is the easiest way to transmit emotion. It is in fact the most commonly used approach. A deck plus a human voiceover has been and continues to be the standard. After spending multiple decades listening to multiple leaders, I have come to the conclusion that most people are only good at verbal communication for very short bursts of time. Most people start sending incorrect emotional signals in about five minutes. Simply put, most managers are bad at long-form verbal communication. This is why I believe managers and leaders need to learn how to write and write well. In my opinion, a well-written document beats a verbal explanation all day, every day. It is also my opinion that learning how to write effectively will eventually make you a better speaker and overall better communicator.

Why Is the Written Word More Powerful than the Spoken Word?

Why is the written word better at creating emotions than the spoken word? It is because our brains are excellent at filling in the blanks. When you are watching someone speak, your brain is processing not just the words coming out of their mouth but also their tone, their facial expressions, their body language, their hand movements, and so on. The person's stage presence heavily influences the emotion the audience feels. The speaker has to nail all of it to make sure the right message and emotion are conveyed to their audience.

Now contrast that with reading a well-written piece of content. Your mind now automatically adds emotion! It adds imagery and color! It adds the background characters! The charisma of the speaker is no longer a factor. Here is a simple exercise. Stand in front of a mirror and read the following sentence aloud to yourself.

"I am truly humbled to be a part of this team! Thank you all for your warm welcome!"

Does gratitude and humility easily come through in your spoken words? Maybe you need to make better eye contact to make it work? Maybe you need to do a little namaste to convey the right emotion? Maybe a softer tone in your speech will help?

Now try silently reading it. The emotion comes through more easily, doesn't it?

The written medium completely outshines the spoken format as the length of the content increases. Extrapolate the same thought exercise from before to a piece of content of about five hundred words. With some editing, the right emotion can be carried throughout those five hundred words. Carrying the right emotion throughout the length of the content is almost impossible in the spoken medium. You have to be like Tony Robbins to nail a five-hundred-word speech. Also, it is a distinct possibility that even after repeated practice sessions in front of the mirror, you might just flub it at the exact moment when you have to speak.

How to Write Well

Now that we have established that the written medium is superior, how does one learn to write well? One word: narratives. Narratives are the best way to convey complex thought with emotion.

PowerPoint decks have decimated our collective ability to write narratives. Bullet points encourage what I call sound-bite thinking. Lazy movie reviews on IMDB are a great example of sound-bite thinking. I am sure you all have seen this before.

"The movie was terrible! I want my money back!"

But what about it was terrible? Was the acting bad? Was the story bad? Was the CGI bad? Was the director Uwe Boll? The fact is, bullet points short-circuit our thinking. Our minds don't think in sound bites. They deal in space operas.

A well-written narrative is similar to a good movie. There is a clear beginning when the lead characters are introduced. Then the plot is introduced where the motives of the main characters are revealed. There is a distinct middle part where the bad guy is introduced, and it ends with an epic battle between the lead characters and the bad guy. To put it simply, if your narrative doesn't have at least three distinct sections—the setup/introduction, core message, ending/call to action—you are doing it wrong.

Here is an example of some good news in a sound-bite format contrasted with a narrative:

Sound bite—Delivered table fixes successfully!

Narrative—The table builder team delivered three usability-related features to customers yesterday (mm/dd/yyyy), which resulted in a 5 percent day 1 decline in P0 customer support tickets, which used to cost the company X dollars in support hours.

The sound bite completely fails to provide any details to the reader, including failing to answer the most important question: So what? So what if the table fixes were delivered successfully?

The narrative, on the other hand, explains the "so what?" and more to the reader without requiring a voiceover from the author.

Here is an example of some bad news in a sound-bite versus narrative format:

Sound bite—Project X's release has slipped to next week, and because of that Project Y's kickoff is delayed as well.

Narrative—The X team discovered a late-breaking release blocker today (mm/dd/yyyy). The team worked over the weekend to fix the bug, but given the severity of the bug (a link to the bug report), they decided to spend a few more days testing to make sure all edge cases are tested. The new release date for Project X is mm/dd/yyyy. This will affect the kickoff of Project Y that was scheduled for this week. The new kickoff date for Project Y is mm/dd/yyyy. We could kick off Project Y earlier if we split resources between Project X and Project Y, but we don't recommend that because the team believes (insert evidence here). Project X is a bigger customer priority than Project Y and splitting resources could further delay Project X's delivery. If leadership disagrees with the decision of swarming on Project X, please contact us.

The sound-bite update will generate a thousand questions. The narrative will generate no further questions. The narrative projects the right emotions to its readers—a sense of urgency from the team, thoughtful decision-making, and a strong point of view of what should be done next.

So how does one write excellent narratives?

One of my all-time favorite authors is Stephen King. I have read all his books, including his nonfiction ones. His nonfiction book *On Writing* is an excellent read for anyone looking to become a better writer. His advice on becoming a great writer is simple: "If you want to be a writer, you must do two things above all others: read a lot and write a lot."[3] It is as simple as that. If you want to become a better writer, take the time to read

---

3   Stephen King, *On Writing: A Memoir of the Craft* (New York: Scribner, 2000), 145.

long-form books and write narratives every week. Just writing five hundred words a week will put you on the path to becoming a good writer. One professional tip—if you want to get better at writing engaging content, read fiction.

Last, get a Grammarly account. It costs the same as your Netflix subscription and will uplevel your writing noticeably almost immediately.

A quick note about GPT and AI-generated content. If you are getting started with long-form narratives, I recommend staying away from GPT until you discover your unique writing style. Every essay I write is uniquely me. It has my unique style, nuances, flaws, and tells that no machine can accurately reproduce until I train it to. Once you have discovered your unique style, you can jump-start your writing with GPT and then add in your unique flair. Personally, I don't use GPT for anything I write because I enjoy the act of writing. If you, the constant reader, didn't guess that, I would be mildly disappointed. Yes, I put a smiley face there, because I felt like it. Will GPT do that? Probably not. I rest my case.

A QUICK RECAP

1. The written word is superior to the spoken word.

2. Good writing is clear and concise. Great writing evokes emotion in the hearts of the reader.

3. Narratives are the best format to convey complex topics.

4. As Stephen King says, "If you want to be a writer, you must do two things above all others: read a lot and write a lot."

5. Use GPT, but give it your unique style. Or maybe don't use GPT for writing at all.

CHAPTER 4

How to Deliver
a Performance
Improvement Plan

I t was 2012, and I was working in Back Bay for a publishing company whose office was in a squat, nondescript, tan-colored building a few blocks away from the Boston Public Library. I remember it was an unusually warm fall morning in Boston. Looking at the people outside, I thought that most of Back Bay had decided to do an impromptu giant picnic to celebrate the unusually nice weather at that time of the year. It seemed like even the birds had paused their migration south to take in the fall glow. It should have been a perfect day, except it wasn't, at least for me. My stomach felt like it was full of lead. I was about to give one of my employees a verbal performance warning for the very first time as an engineering manager. I felt like I was the one about to be given a warning.

Since the time I decided to become an engineering manager, I had decided that I was going to do all my one-on-ones outside as much as possible. I had decided to break this news to the employee in this one-on-one. Bob[4] and I stepped out into the Boston sun and started going down our regular one-on-one route. We typically walked to the Boston Public Library, looped around the Prudential Mall, and made our way back to work. We had looped around the mall, but I still hadn't mustered the courage to tell Bob the bad news. When we were only a block away from our office building, I finally blurted out the bad news to him in a spectacularly unprofessional manner. I said something along the lines of, "Your tech lead told me that you are not showing up to the scrum meetings, so I have decided to put you in a performance improvement plan." After I said those words, I realized how terrible it was, and I just wanted to fold into myself and disappear from existence.

This was mistake number one. I had skipped the formal verbal warning part and had gone straight to the written warning, which was unfair to Bob. I had given Bob some feedback about his performance, but I never emphasized the seriousness of the issue, because I was too chicken to say the right words.

Bob stopped dead in his tracks and looked at me with his brows scrunched in confusion and anger. "You're putting me on a performance improvement plan for not showing up to a couple of meetings?" asked Bob.

Mistake number two was not leading with the most important area of improvement. There were a lot more issues with Bob besides not showing up to meetings. I simply hadn't taken the time to write down all my talking points, and I hadn't practiced my script. So, what I delivered was some of the feedback, but not

---

4   This is a pseudonym.

all, and certainly not the most important one. I then backtracked and started talking about the bigger performance issues, which were all centered on not hitting commitments.

Bob then started pointing blame at others in the team, including his tech lead and neighboring teams. This time I did the right thing and pulled the conversation back to him and his areas of improvement, not the teams.

"Why did you not mention this to me before?! I want to talk to HR; this doesn't make any sense to me," said Bob angrily and stormed away, leaving me looking at the October sky and wondering how I had managed to mangle this conversation so badly.

I walked back slowly to my cube, making sure I didn't accidentally run into Bob, and sat down. I was extremely thankful for the high walls of my cube.

Compartmentalization

When I ask aspiring engineering managers how they feel about delivering a bad performance review, the answers I typically get are variations of, "Yes, it is a necessary thing, and I have no problem doing it," "Yeah, it will be tough, but I will figure it out," and so on. Most people severely underestimate how mentally exhausting delivering a poor performance review will be.

Most people attach the measure of their self-worth to how they perform at work,[5] which is sad, but that's the reality. A bad performance review directly affects their sense of self-worth;

---

5   Lora E. Park and Jennifer Crocker, "Contingencies of Self-Worth and Responses to Negative Interpersonal Feedback," *Self and Identity* 7, no. 2 (2008): 184–203.

unsurprisingly, their reaction is often negative. Imagine telling a child that they suck at [insert favorite sport or subject]. How do you think they will react? Now imagine telling it to a grown-up who typically has a smaller support system than most children do. Children respond to this with sadness and look for comfort from adults. Some adults will react to events like this with panic and anger and could lash out at the person delivering the message. There is no way to make this event an unemotional one, but there are a few things that you, as their manager, can do to reduce the emotional drain on both parties.

The common advice given to managers is to build emotional intelligence, that important skill of recognizing, understanding, and managing our own emotions in positive ways while also recognizing the emotions of others. However, an equally important skill to sharpen is compartmentalization. Compartmentalization, in this context, is the ability to get through individual work situations (and the associated emotions) without letting it affect other subsequent work. In your career as a manager, you will be attacked, accused, ridiculed, critiqued, and, in rare cases, yelled at by various people as you deliver bad news. To survive as a manager, you must develop your ability to compartmentalize events and feedback. You can't let it "get" to you. Of course, that's easy to say, but hard to achieve in practice. I don't consider myself particularly good at it, but I will list some resources in the appendix that have helped me.

Typically, the road that leads to the tough conversation goes through two major milestones. The first milestone is the verbal warning, and the second is the official written warning (the notorious performance improvement plan, infamously known as the PIP). So let's walk through this rocky road.

Verbal Warning

Managers rarely detect performance issues directly because they are not in the day-to-day, or at least they shouldn't be. The best way to get wind of potential performance issues in your team is to stay close to the people who care most about delivering the outcomes your team is driving toward. In most cases, they are the employees on your team and stakeholders outside your team who are typically product managers. Staying close means regular one-on-ones with everyone on your team and everyone your team is directly working with. The key question you should ask in those one-on-ones is, "What potential risks or roadblocks can you think of?" Most people won't tell you upfront that person X is not pulling their weight. However, if you continually work to build trust with your team and stakeholders, at some point, somebody will give a gentle hint about somebody not pulling their weight.

Performance issues typically come in two sour flavors: not competent in skills required for the job or not competent in the company's culture. If it's a skills issue, the signals to look for are consistently falling behind schedule and needing more than usual help from the team to finish tasks. If you do regular one-on-ones with your extended team, you will likely be able to realize this easily. It is also okay to ask variations of, "How is person X doing? I noticed they were behind schedule." If you do this enough (asking everyone about everyone and everything), you will notice patterns emerging.

The key thing to remember while collecting feedback is to never explicitly "out" someone at this stage. When collecting feedback, ask about everyone. Don't make it look like you are specifically trying to determine if person X has a performance issue. However, if this person gets past this stage into the next stage, then you have to ask exactly if their performance is getting better.

If it's a culture fit issue, the signals to look for are not taking feedback well, not being willing to disagree and commit, publicly berating peers or stakeholders, and, the strongest signal of all, not showing up. Culture fit issues take longer to manifest themselves, but they are hard to miss when they do. If you are plugged into regular meetings where the team exchanges ideas and statuses, you should be able to recognize who is having a tough time fitting in.

Once you have observed (or indirectly observed with supporting evidence) multiple infractions (three is the rule I recommend), it is time to act on the employee. Let's call this employee Bob. Before you say anything to him, write down these three things:

1. Where is he falling short (missing deadlines, being unpleasant to others, etc.)?

2. Who else has noticed this behavior?

3. What are things he needs to do to get better?

This document is not for Bob, at least for now. For now, this is to help you prepare yourself for the first tough conversation and to make sure you have the conviction that there is, in fact, a problem that needs to be dealt with. To put it simply, if most of the people around Bob don't like working with him, you have a problem.

Now you are ready for the first tough conversation. *Do not* schedule a separate meeting for this conversation. All this will do is drive up Bob's anxiety leading up to it and increase potential background chatter within your team. Instead, use one of your regular one-on-ones to have this conversation. Most of my one-on-ones are scheduled for either thirty minutes or forty-five minutes. I recommend not going beyond forty-five minutes for any one-on-one. The action starts and ends in the first thirty.

Once the meeting starts, *do not* spend the first fifteen minutes exchanging pleasantries. Start it along these lines:

> Hey, Bob. I wanted to share some not-so-great feedback about your recent work performance. Now, before we get going, I want you to know that this is not a "let's fire Bob" conversation. *I still firmly believe that you can succeed here long-term* if you fix some of the issues we are about to discuss.

Notice how this fictional conversation offers both caution and reassurance for Bob. You, as a manager, *have* to convince Bob that you believe in his long-term success in your team. I recommend you say it multiple times during the conversation. You *must* believe that Bob can turn it around. Then get into the details of the issue itself. Be as specific as possible. "You have consistently missed deadlines. For example, here, here, and here," "Your teammates feel they can't give you honest feedback because you become defensive," "Your teammates feel they have to help you out more than needed for someone in your role and level," and so on. Invariably Bob will ask about the specifics of who gave the feedback. *Do not* share the specifics of who gave the feedback. Most of the time, when managers share specifics, conversations devolve into shifting blame to others, and that is not productive.

At this point, one of two things can happen. Either Bob says, "Oh, man, I didn't realize that my performance was slipping. How can I get better?" Or he starts becoming defensive and tries to justify his poor performance (usually by blaming others) or by not accepting the feedback completely. If the person accepts the feedback, you are golden for now. Let them know what changes you want to see, how you will evaluate the results, and a time frame around it.

If the person starts to become defensive and blame others, quickly interrupt with something like this:

> Bob, this conversation is about you, not the rest of your team. We can dig into the specifics of each situation if needed in subsequent conversations. Still, I want you to understand that multiple people in your team and outside your team have shared the same feedback about you, and I expect you to work on it and fix it.

There is a natural power imbalance between you as a manager and your employees, and 99.9 percent of the time, you shouldn't lean into that imbalance. But in situations like these, it is completely appropriate to lean into that and make it clear to employees what they need to fix if they hope to continue working in your team.

In some cases, there will be situations where a person might be culturally a great fit but not a great fit from a skills standpoint (e.g., back-end development in a mostly front-end product team). In those cases, it is okay to explore moving them to a different team (the employee should also be aligned with the move). However, if you end up taking that route, I highly recommend a mini-interview with the other team to assess the skills match before officially moving that person.

There will also be situations when the person is going through a rough patch in life, and their work is taking a hit because of it. In those situations, make it clear to them that you empathize with them. Give them time off, a lighter workload, special mental health support, or anything else you think will help them navigate the situation. However, you do have to put a timeline around it. If you don't, your boss will.

But if they continue to reject your feedback and point blame at everyone else besides themselves, then end the conversation with something like this:

Clearly, your team and I disagree with your assessment of what is happening. I believe in the team around you, and I can't fire them all to accommodate your needs. Let's stop this conversation now, but think seriously about what you want to do next. Next time we meet, if you still believe that there is nothing you could have done better or differently, then we should start discussing your exit from the company. I also understand that this is an extremely stressful situation for you, and if you want to take some time to reflect on things and have a follow-up conversation, it is totally all right.

This is the end of the first conversation. After the meeting, recap the conversation in an email and send it to the employee and make sure your HR person is copied on the email. If the employee has accepted the feedback, then schedule regular check-ins to make sure the employee's progress is aligned with their performance goals.

If the meeting ended with the employee not fully accepting the feedback and the next steps, specifically call it out in the email and pencil in a date for a follow-up. In the follow-up, if the employee is still not convinced that anything is wrong with their performance, then you need to start collectively figuring out an exit date (from the company) for that employee.

Last, document all of this with your HR person. In this phase, the only time you need to include the HR person in your conversation is when/if the employee rejects the feedback and is convinced that they are right and everyone else is wrong. In general, try to keep HR out from the meeting itself primarily because it will increase the anxiety level in the room, but keep them in the loop at all times by copying them in all your emails.

A QUICK RECAP

1. Spend time with *everyone* to learn about performance issues earlier.

2. Repurpose a one-on-one meeting to share feedback with the employee.

3. Keep the anxiety level low in that meeting.

4. Reiterate to the employee that you still believe that they can succeed in your team.

5. Lean into your authority when needed (if the employee doesn't want to change).

6. Keep HR out of the meetings, but keep them informed.

7. Remember that the situation is salvageable at this phase.

8. Timebox (use time constraints) all activities.

9. *Document everything.*

Celebrate with a beverage of choice, and let's move on to the next rocky milestone.

Written Warning (Performance Improvement Plan)

After the verbal warning, I recommend monitoring the employee's performance for about sixty days. If you consistently see better performance, you never enter the next phase. The only way to determine if an employee is consistently improving is to collect quantitative (e.g., consistently hitting commitments) and qualitative (e.g., interviews) feedback from everybody in the employee's orbit. Are they hitting all their time commitments? Are they showing up? Are their colleagues sharing positive feedback about them? If most of the answers to those questions are true, congratulate the employee on the performance and remove them from under your microscope. However, if you don't see meaningful improvement in the first thirty days, you must go to the written warning phase. Now our previous discussions of knowing your audience and crafting carefully written communications begin to pay dividends.

I'm going to assume you've internalized those recommendations and can draw on them as you craft the written warning and improvement plan discussed next.

As a manager, I typically see 50 percent of employees who go through the first phase (verbal warning) enter the written warning phase, and it becomes progressively worse. Much worse. This is when you should prepare to manage the employee out of the company. Sorry to break it to you, but those are the facts!

Once you have decided that Bob is not improving, set up a meeting to explicitly discuss his performance, and this time you need HR in the room. Before the meeting, document where you expected better performance from him and are not seeing it as evidenced by X (pull requests, teammate feedback, stakeholder feedback, etc.). Review your document with HR and send the document to the employee for review before the meeting. Last, give yourself enough time to mentally prepare for this meeting, as it will be tough.

Once the meeting kicks off, explain the agenda to the employee. I recommend the agenda to be along the lines of, "Hey, Bob. I haven't seen a consistent change in your behavior. The document I sent you has all the details about your inconsistent performance. We can discuss the document's details in this meeting if you have questions. We will also discuss the next steps."

Most employees who enter this phase do not make it through. This is why I typically give the employee a peaceful and easy way out of the company at this stage. Before I get into the written document, *I ask them if they really want to go through with this or if they want to leave the company with severance.* In most cases, I offer employees two months of severance pay, including health insurance coverage for those months. If the person is in a leadership role, I typically offer them three months of paid severance and six months of paid health insurance. Because I am offering severance, HR needs to be in the room to answer any employee questions. Also, whatever you are planning on offering, discuss it with HR before the meeting to make sure you are generally aligned on the size of the severance package.

Note that I only offer this option to employees who are not actively poisoning the well. If the employee is actively causing disruption, you must move quickly and get them out of the company without severance. Ninety percent of employees take the exit package if given the option, and the other 10 percent will negotiate the severance terms after the meeting. Be more flexible on the health insurance than the cash component. Your HR partner will likely be able to guide you through this. However, don't be afraid to say, "Sorry, we can't do anything more than this." Your goal at this stage is not to save the employee but to give them a soft landing outside the company.

As you discuss all this with the employee, make it abundantly clear that this improvement plan reflects not their overall skills or attitude but a mismatch between their skills and personality with the company. Make it clear to them that you believe they will be successful in another company. You will not get this part right on your first attempt, but over time you will.

If the employee doesn't want to take the exit offer, walk them through the document you prepared and the outcomes you are looking for. Also, let them know that if you don't see a dramatic change in the next thirty days, they will have to exit the company without severance. You will have to monitor their output almost daily, document it, and share it regularly with the employee and the HR person. So I recommend clearing your calendar as much as possible for the next thirty days. While it is possible that things will improve, you should start preparing for an exit.

A QUICK RECAP

1. Most employees don't make it through the process if they have reached this stage.

2. Keep your HR partner in the loop and in all meetings with the employee.

3. Write a concise document that captures the expected outcomes, lack of progress, and supporting evidence from teammates and stakeholders.

4. Set up a meeting with the employee to walk through the document. This time your HR person should be in the room.

5. Offer a severance package (salary and health coverage) early on in the meeting and give the employee an easy way out.

6. Be open to negotiating the terms of the severance package.

7. Reiterate to them that everything happening is not an overall reflection of their competency but rather a mismatch between their skills and your company's needs.

8. If the employee still insists on going through with the process, let them know that they have thirty days to show a dramatic behavior change, that you will monitor their output daily, and make it clear that if their performance doesn't improve in thirty days, they will have to exit the company without a severance.

9. If the employee has chosen the eighth point, clear your calendar and mentally prepare yourself to document outputs and behaviors daily.

Your goal in this phase is to convince the employee to take the severance, which most people will do without needing a lot of convincing, but fully expect an emotionally draining back-and-forth with the employee during this phase.

The Exit

This phase is for when everything has failed. Ominous, for sure, but thankfully, this is also the shortest phase of this journey. Most employees who get to this phase will not show a sudden unexpected jump in performance. Miracles do happen once in a while. Though it hasn't happened to me yet, since my career is not over, maybe one day it will. Assuming a miracle hasn't happened, set up a meeting with the employee on the thirty-day mark with HR in the room. Keep the meeting to thirty minutes and deliver the bad news to the employee straight. Something along these lines:

Based on your documented performance that I have been sharing with you regularly, I have decided that you are not a good fit for the company, and I have decided to let you go. Your last date will be X, and HR will walk you through the logistics after this conversation. As I shared with you before, just because you are not a good fit for this company doesn't mean you won't excel in a different company with a different team. I am also willing to be your reference as you look for future job opportunities.

Pause briefly for questions, and end the meeting. Once the employee officially agrees on an exit date, also work out the details of who will announce the departure to the team.

If the employee is an individual contributor, you, as a manager, should make all the announcements. If the employee is in a leadership role, allow them to break the news to their team, but you need to be aligned on what they will share with their team, and if possible, you should be in the room when they make the announcement to their team. When individuals on your team ask what happened, share as little as possible. Say something along the lines of, "Bob and I decided that his skills weren't a great match for the company, so he has decided to pursue external opportunities."

The reason behind sharing very little is to give the employee a clean break. It would be best if you weren't trash-talking the employee in front of anyone because the business world is small, and there is a distinct possibility that Bob might end up working with some of his ex-teammates in a different company. In that company, Bob might actually be doing well.

After the employee departs, you are done. At this point, if you feel like a small part of your soul has died in the process, congratulations, you are a normal person. Coaching people through performance issues is hard, but letting people go is harder.[6] Always remember that your employees are real people. They have feelings, families, dreams, and aspirations. So always be kind, fair, helpful, and objective as much as possible.

A QUICK RECAP

1. At this stage, the employee's performance usually won't change dramatically.

2. If you have decided to let the employee go, do it in a thirty-minute meeting.

3. Keep the meeting short and to the point.

4. Own the message and the decision.

5. Don't trash-talk the employee in front of the broader team.

6. Be kind.

---

6   Rebecca Knight, "How to Decide Whether to Fire Someone," *Harvard Business Review*, January 28, 2019, https://hbr.org/2019/01/how-to-decide -whether-to-fire-someone.

CHAPTER 5

How to Deliver
Bad News to Stakeholders

By 2019 I was firmly in middle management. Our offices were in an old, chilly brownstone right next to Chinatown in Boston. Back then, I was managing a team of about fifty, and I also had managers reporting to me. Additionally, I was in line for a promotion into an executive role. I had also recently ditched my L.L.Bean shirts for Bonobos. I was moving up the corporate ladder and life was great. However, to prove that I could actually do the job, I was put in charge of a large project that was a key goal for the COO, who worked out of the Seattle office. To get a seat at the executive table, almost everyone currently at the table will have to say yes to your promotion packet, so it was important for this C-level executive to have faith in me.

One thing to point out about COOs is that they are driven by numbers. In general, COOs, CFOs, and CROs and their teams are highly predictable. You add X number of salespeople, you get Y revenue out of it. Conversely, product and engineering organizations are not highly predictable because there is a fair bit of creativity involved in creating features, designing them, and shipping them. It's hard to put a precise timebox around a creative endeavor.

The beginning of the project was great. Everybody involved in it was energized by the prospect of working on a critical company project. As the project kicked off, everybody at the top wanted to know when the project would be delivered. As a team we had done some rough estimation of the timelines, just for internal planning purposes, and I shared that number with the COO and caveated it heavily. The date made its way into a deck that was presented to the CEO, and in that meeting that rough estimate became a firm date. This was mistake number one. I should have broken the large project into smaller customer-facing milestones and shared the dates for only the early milestones that we as a team had confidence in.

After about three months, it was clear that my team would not be able to hit the deadline that we committed to. They told me that they would need six more months. I got on a call with the COO and let them know that we were going to be late and committed to coming up with a new plan in a week. I remember eating breakfast, lunch, and dinner with my team that week. At the end of the week, we got a new plan, and I decided to walk through the plan in person with the COO.

I remember stepping out of Seattle-Tacoma Airport into a downpour, which was slightly different than the usual Seattle drizzle. Normally, I would fly into Seattle on a Sunday, relax overnight, and then head to the mothership bright and early the next morning. However, this time around I couldn't find any Sunday night flights, because of the short notice. So I walked out of Sea-Tac, got into an Uber, and headed straight for the headquarters.

My nerves were fine for the trip to the office, but as soon as I stepped into the shiny Seattle building, my heart started thumping a tad bit faster. By this point in my career, I had delivered project delays to numerous stakeholders many times, but this was the first time I had to deliver bad news to an executive. Not just any executive but an executive who could easily fire me on the spot. By the time I got to the right floor, my heart was trip-hammering, my mouth was dry, and there was a general sense of dread. It was like going to the principal's office, but worse. Delivering bad news is one of those things that only gets easier over time. Like, slightly easier.

As soon as I stepped into his office, I could tell the COO was not in a great mood. He sat hunched forward in his desk, hands clasped together, and glared at me as I sat down. The first thing I said after I sat down was, "This is my fault. I take ownership of the delay." Those were the magic words. Actually, those are *the* magic words for anybody reading. As soon as I said those words, his demeanor changed instantly. He relaxed his body, leaned forward, and asked me, "How do we set this right?" He didn't ask me how I was going to fix it; instead he offered to help me get this train back on the right track. Showing accountability and ownership are critically important to build your credibility as a leader.

I walked him through the various milestones of the project and how I planned to add more people on the team to make sure the project didn't slip again. I also convinced him to spend more time with the Boston team and help rally the team, which he did, and the team loved him for doing that. When the project shipped, the team had built a personal connection with the COO and understood his motivations. The COO understood the complexity of the project and also was able to appreciate the hard work the team was putting into the project.

The project did slip a couple of times, but the team was able to get it back on track with a combination of cutting scope a bit and good old elbow grease. In the end the project shipped on the date we committed to. Oh, and remember the promotion I mentioned? Yeah, that didn't happen. What did you all think this was, a Hallmark movie?

Project Delays Are Like Death and Taxes

Project deadlines and delays are like death and taxes. Inevitable. There will be times when you, as a manager of a team, will have to deliver bad news to your stakeholders. The most common bad news you will have to deliver is delayed projects. One might think, "What is the big deal about delays? It's not like people are dying because of them!"

In most cases, that is true, but the politics around projects and delivery will have a meaningful impact on your long-term trajectory in the company, including affecting future raises and promotions. To be successful as a manager, you must master the art of delivering bad news, sometimes even to the CEO. One point to note is that when I refer to projects, I am referring to large initiatives that take multiple months to finish and have multiple stakeholders. To understand the nuances, let's begin with how projects come about. Also, I interchangeably use "executive," "project sponsor," and "executive sponsor" in this chapter. They all refer to the person who funded the initiative.

People are the most expensive line item for any company. Most new managers don't get this, but at the core, people leaders need to think like investment managers. Where do I deploy these smart people who will result in positive revenue gain for the company and its shareholders? Every year, the leaders at the top of the company have to debate (often spiritedly) and align on where to spend the company's money, in other words, their team's time. These debates are zero-sum games because the budget available to the company is fixed. Often, an executive will fund their project at the expense of someone else's budget. This executive is now on the hook for delivering the project on a timely basis and for the revenue generated by that project. If this project fails, the executive will be in the hot seat and have to answer some tough questions, and the person they stole the budget from will make sure the tough questions are really tough. The executive on the hook will pass the pressure down to the teams responsible for delivering the project.

Building Trust with Senior Leadership

If you have been trusted to deliver a key initiative, you must build social capital with the person funding the initiative. You will need it when you have to deliver bad news to them. The best way to build trust with any senior leader is transparency. Most senior leaders are hungry for information, so include them in regular status updates. Actively track risk and mitigation steps and socialize them with the stakeholders. Do regular one-on-one meetings with all key stakeholders. Write weekly summaries of the project status, risk mitigation strategies, and any feature trade-off details and send them to the stakeholders. Project statuses should contain a high-level summary of how the project is progressing and whether the project is still on track to hit its previously committed delivery date or not. A risk mitigation summary should include any potential risks you can foresee. For example, if your project requires your legal department to sign off on the scope and they are dragging their feet, then that is a risk worth calling out in your summary. Trade-off details are your proposed changes to scope to hit the deadline. For example, if a last-minute change of scope is dumped on your project, it is worth asking the question if that scope is really needed when the project is released or if it can be a fast follow-on addition.

Additionally, highlight where you need the senior leader's help in every weekly summary: examples, resourcing, conflicts with other business units, and so on. Simply put, make it easy for the sponsoring leader to report information to their bosses and clarify where they can help with the project. One tip: you don't want the senior leader involved in your day-to-day unless you really need them to intervene, which is usually when you run into issues with other organizations. So choose wisely.

Also, build camaraderie between your team and the stakeholders. Push the executive to hang out with your team in low-pressure situations and vice versa: lunches, dinners, drinks, and so on. Major project milestone celebrations are a great way to get people to socialize in person. Make sure the executive knows most of your team by name, especially the leaders on your team. And make sure your team hears from the executive directly about the importance of the project they are working on. You are making sure everyone understands each other's context, and this humanizes everybody. It is easy to get mad at a talking head on Zoom, but getting angry at someone you had lunch with is tough.

Delivering the Bad News to Stakeholders

Okay, so your team tells you they are going to be late. You have trimmed the scope as much as you can, but still, the project will be delayed, and now you have to tell the sponsor the bad news. If the project is delayed only by a few weeks, strongly consider asking your team to work extra to get the project over the finish line on time. Also, consider leaning on your peers and asking them for resourcing help to complete the project. Will getting the project out on time make a meaningful difference to the company's future? Probably not. However, it will dramatically increase the project sponsor's trust in your team and you as a leader. The more trust the company leaders have in your team, the better the opportunities that will come your team's way, which will, in turn, buoy everyone's careers.

If a few working nights and weekends won't deliver the project on time, then a one-on-one sit-down with the sponsor is needed. As much as possible, do the meeting in person. Remote work has made this slightly challenging for many companies, but nothing breeds more trust than a face-to-face meeting where you can look the other person in the eye, take ownership of the message, and deliver bad news. In my career, I have flown across the country to deliver bad news to my stakeholders.

However, before you walk into the meeting, here are a few discussion points that will come up in the conversation that you should be prepared for:

- The number one question to expect from your project sponsor is, "Why did this happen? What caused this?" Be prepared with the root cause (incorrect estimation, customer feedback, etc.), but *do not* pin the blame on any person. Put the blame on yourself and take accountability. Own the failure.

- Be prepared to answer what you will do differently next time around. If incorrect estimations caused the delay, lean on others to validate your team's assumptions. If late customer feedback caused the delay, consider socializing smaller changes more often with customers and getting feedback. Or your team may need engineers with different skills, for example, back end versus front end. The bottom line is to be prepared with clear next steps on what drastic changes you will make to salvage the project.

- Come prepared with the new timeline, including milestones. Do not present just one final date. Present multiple milestones, the customer benefit at each milestone, the dates of those milestones, and your confidence level associated with each milestone. You should have higher confidence in a milestone a month out than one three months out. *Do not* walk into the conversation without a confidence level on your dates.

- Be prepared to deal with rhetorical questions like, "Is the team working hard enough?" or "Does the team know the importance of this project?" and so on. This is the project sponsor venting, nothing more. There are no real answers to this except saying yes and refocusing the conversation on the path forward.

In the meeting, start by taking ownership of the delay. Then get into the previous bullet points without needing to be prompted by the other person. Once you have gotten through your narrative, as much as possible, focus more on the path forward than the past, but don't try to deflect any questions. The key feeling you want to present here to the project sponsor is that the pressure they are feeling is shared equally by you and your team, and you will do your best to deliver this project on the new timeline. Additionally, offer to be in the room when the executive has to share the news about the delay with the people above them, the CEO, the board, and so on. The executive will most likely refuse, but the act will highlight your ownership. If you have built trust with your project sponsor and have all your talking points in order, and if you show the right level of urgency to see this through, you will survive with your credibility intact.

Meeting Your Commitments

Many of you might be wondering, "Shouldn't leaders create a safe space for failures to happen?" Broadly speaking, yes, it is true, and you, as a people leader, should create a safe space for your team to experiment and fail. However, repeated failures will never end well for anybody. Your team can't be working on failed science experiments most of the time. Most of the time, they should provide value to the customers who buy your products. As a manager, you must make sure your team is contributing positively to the company's bottom line. Anybody who says, "It's okay to fail as long as you learn from it," hasn't worked in a real company. A more accurate version of that phrase is, "It is okay to fail as long as, over time, you deliver value to the company."

Another big reason for you as a manager to honor your commitments is to build trust with the people funding your project, the leaders at the top. Some of you are probably thinking, "Aren't the best executives servant leaders? Shouldn't they be serving us?" Yes, all of that is true. The best executive leaders are, in fact, servant leaders. However, the hard cold reality is corporations are capitalist institutions, including the one you work at. They exist to return positive returns to their shareholders and add customer value. That means someone (private investors, public shareholders, etc.) is giving your company money and they expect to get an outsize return on their investment. *All* the leaders who are in executive seats deeply understand that fundamental truth. They have to tell their investors how they are working to put their investments to work. They have to share with them the projects they are spinning up, when they will be delivered, and how they will positively affect the bottom line. The more you can showcase to your bosses that you understand this reality, the more convinced they will become that you will succeed as a leader.

The last big reason teams need to consistently deliver products and features used by customers is to build their self-confidence. When customers use the features delivered by your team, it validates their work and, in fact, their existence. Teams that don't deliver for an extended period will get disillusioned over time and lose interest in their work. Those teams also become prime cost-cutting targets when the budget tightens. Yes, another cold hard reality.

A QUICK RECAP

1. Build trust with your executive leader and other stakeholders.

2. When projects get delayed, own the messaging.

3. Deliver the message in a face-to-face, one-on-one meeting.

4. Come prepared with specifics about how you will deliver on the new timeline.

5. Share and show the urgency of your project sponsor.

6. Be ready to ask your team to work extra if you think it will help the team deliver on time.

7. Understand that corporations are capitalist institutions.

8. Teams that don't deliver value consistently will disappear over time.

CHAPTER 6

How to Deliver
Bad News to Customers:
Project Delays

This was sometime in 2019 when I was a newly minted executive. I was still working out of the perpetually chilly brownstone near Chinatown, but I had the fancy title of vice president, engineering. However, I seemed to spend more and more time putting out fires, and a three-alarm fire was about to land on my desk.

The company I worked for sold enterprise software. This meant that our customers were other companies, not individuals. One of my teams was on the hook for delivering a feature that a very high-profile customer was waiting for. We had committed a soft timeline (we were 50 percent confident) for that feature to the account rep who was managing that customer. Timelines are magical in nature. When you share a date with somebody else, they change. What we thought was a soft timeline had become a hard deadline for the account rep and, through him, for the customer as well. In hindsight, I should have never shared a soft timeline, but the account rep wanted some date from me even if it wasn't super accurate, so I caved. He was a charismatic sales guy, after all. This is probably the spark that lit the fuse that eventually bloomed into a raging forest fire in about three weeks.

That date came and went, and my team couldn't deliver that feature. We had a spate of stability issues in production, and I refocused my team to center on that, and we dropped all feature development work. I kept the account rep in the loop with all the decisions my team was making, including the decision to delay the project. Judging by his spiffy responses, I had assumed he and the customer were okay with the new delivery dates. Then I got the call from the CPO.

The CPO called me around 8:00 p.m. as I was making my way home on the much-hated Green Line subway that seemed to be always filled with human sardines. He let me know that the high-profile customer was furious about the missed deadline and was demanding an explanation as to what happened. He told me that they might be an attrition risk and told me to be ready for a call at 8:00 p.m. the next day with the customer. If we lost that customer, I was pretty sure heads would roll.

I spent most of the next day collecting as much information about the customer as possible. I found out more details about their current pain point that the feature would solve. I pored through the customer support tickets they had created. I spent time with all the sales and support people who had interacted with individuals from that company in the last year. I looked up all the people who were attending the 8:00 p.m. meeting, found their profiles on LinkedIn, and memorized all their names and faces. If you ever want to build instant rapport with someone you just met, use their first name to address them for the rest of the conversation. A person's name is the sweetest sound for them.[7]

At the end of the day, I got on the customer call. There were about ten people from my side, half from sales and half from support, but all in various levels of nervousness. Three people from the customer's side were all in various states of anger and disappointment. The account rep kicked off the call and tried to lighten the mood. He knew that the VP from the customer side liked football, so he launched into a pretty entertaining soliloquy about the New England Patriots. About thirty seconds later, the VP brusquely interrupted the account rep and said, "Enough of that; can one of you explain why you can't deliver what you promised?" He emphasized the word "promise." His choice of words had the intended effect. The account rep mumbled a quick apology and quickly handed it over to me.

I started off by apologizing and owning the delay in the initiative. I walked them through my own reasons to push the deadline out. I explained to them in detail the stability issues we were seeing in production and how it was important to address those before taking on feature work. All the time, I took care to address them by their first names, especially the VP from the other side. I emphasized on the fact that worsening stability in our production systems would also affect them as users of the

---

7   Dale Carnegie, "Remember Names to Build Better Professional Relationships," accessed March 28, 2024, https://www.dalecarnegie.com/en/courses/262.

platform. Finally, I told them the new date that we were tracking toward and asked them if that new date was acceptable, and said a silent prayer.

The VP had softened considerably by then. He empathized with my team's situation, agreed that the stability of the system was important, and thanked me for providing them with a detailed explanation. Then he very politely said that the new date was unacceptable.

Thankfully, I had a plan B that I had worked out with the professional services team. Plan B was to build a custom one-off solution for this customer in the event they balked at the new date. Custom one-off customer solutions have a high long-term cost of ownership. Now, every time you add a feature to your core product, you have to make sure all one-off solutions work as well. Typically, the professional services team would charge customers for any custom work, but the professional services team agreed to waive the charges for this specific customer.

Thankfully the customer accepted my plan B. First names and a little bit of providence saved the day. The three big takeaways—always take responsibility and never deflect blame, give your customers the gory details, and always have a plan B, C, and D.

The Major Types of Customers

Most companies make money by selling something of value to customers: software, services, devices, and so forth. Understandably, when those products don't work, customers get upset. Depending on who your company is selling to, you will get different levels of frustration from customers when things break. The strategy for delivering bad news also differs depending on customer type. Let's break down the major types of customers first.

First up, individual consumers. These are people like you and me who buy technology-enabled products (like streaming, productivity software, etc.) for personal use, and, according to *Forbes*, the dollars we spend on these products typically range from around $500 to $1,000 per year.[8] Companies that cater to individual consumers are commonly known as consumer businesses. Some examples of consumer businesses are Netflix, Amazon Prime, and Apple.

Next up, enterprise customers. These are large companies that buy products and services for commercial purposes. Enterprise customers tend to spend millions (and in some cases billions) of dollars every year on products and services. Examples of companies that sell to enterprise customers are IBM, Microsoft, Amazon Web Services, and Salesforce. Note that some of these companies have consumer businesses as well. For example, Microsoft sells tablets to consumers and Office 365 products to enterprises.

Last, small and medium businesses, or SMBs. These are smaller enterprise companies with a staff of mostly one or two employees, including the founders. They typically spend around $1,000 to $10,000 per year on products and services. Examples of companies that sell to SMBs are Airtable, Asana, Squarespace, and Patreon.

---

8   Geraldine Orentas, "Streaming Trends for 2024: 44% Report Streaming Costs Increasing over the Last Year," *Forbes*, February 23, 2024, https://www.forbes.com/home-improvement/internet/streaming-survey/.

Ostensibly, one might think that the customers spending the most on products will complain the loudest, but that is not necessarily true. The group of customers that complain the loudest are typically SMBs, primarily because any impact to their operations directly affects their bottom line in a meaningful way and because SMBs don't have redundancies in their operations. SMBs count each dollar they make and are very careful about where to spend it.

There are generally two types of bad news you might have to deliver to customers: missed deadlines on commitments (you promised them feature X by date Y) or why something is not working as it's supposed to. Missed deadlines on commitments are typically not a huge deal for consumer-focused companies. It really doesn't matter to the end customer if the new season of *Stranger Things* is delayed by a few weeks. For enterprises and SMBs, they do matter. They typically matter in situations when their original buying decision was influenced by your commitment to delivering a feature that they really want, or they want a specific feature or bug-fix delivered because it is affecting their day-to-day operations. If you hear from your bosses that the customer wants a meeting to talk about the delays in the timeline, volunteer to be in the meeting to deliver the news to them. If you want to build a career in leadership, get used to owning and navigating messy situations. In fact, volunteer for them.

Understanding Your Customers

Before you get into a meeting with your enterprise customer (SMBs or large), the single biggest thing to understand is their pain. What are they not able to achieve because they don't have the feature they requested? How much revenue are they losing every day because a specific bug hasn't been fixed? How many person hours are they wasting because of the delay? You have to be able to genuinely empathize with your customer if you hope to prevent them from dumping your product and moving on to a competitor. The only way to do that is to understand your customer in detail.

The easiest way to figure out what a specific customer cares about is to talk to your customer support and success teams. Those teams typically interact with customers more frequently than product development teams and therefore are a rich source of information about the customers, their road maps, and their pain points. Additionally, also brainstorm with your internal team about potential work-arounds that might help satisfy the customer needs. It is completely okay to deploy one-off solutions for your enterprise customers, and yes, I will fight you on that. Last, work out a new timeline for delivery and make sure you are aligned with your internal team on it. Now, you are ready for the meeting with the enterprise customer.

The meetings are typically filled with a lot of people from both sides. There will be leaders from both your company and the customer. The various leaders from the customer company are on the call to emphasize the point that the feature you failed to deliver is extremely important to them, and the leaders from your side are on the call to make sure they don't lose that customer. The customer doesn't care much about what anyone from your side has to say, except you as the manager of the team who is working to get their feature out. They want to hear from you, not from the sales leader or the customer success leader or even your boss. They want to hear the details directly from the person who was in charge of delivering the feature to them.

When it is your turn to speak, introduce yourself and start off by apologizing for the delays and own the delay. If you have done your homework, you will know why they were looking forward to that specific feature, so reiterate to them that you understand their situation and empathize. Just by sharing with them what you know about their business goals goes a long way with any customer. It shows that you care about the success of their business. After that, get into the specifics of what caused the delay. If your team underestimated the size of the effort, share those gory details with your customer. Depending on how technical your customer is, they might or might not understand the details, but they will tremendously appreciate you for sharing those details. In the end, most customers are only looking for transparency.

If the delay was caused by a prioritization change, the message is a bit trickier to deliver. You don't want to give the impression that other customers are more important. However, one thing to keep in mind is, most enterprise customers *also* have to deal with shifting priorities and limited resources, so use that to your advantage. Your message should be something along these lines:

> The big reason for the delay was resourcing challenges on our side. You all can probably empathize a bit here as I am sure you all deal with competing priorities all the time. No company has all the resources to do all the work.

If delivered with humility and empathy, most customers will understand your situation. In the end, most customers just want to hear the message directly from the team working on the feature and not from the sales leader.

Finally, follow it up with a new delivery date and volunteer to set up weekly syncs with the customer team to keep them up to date on the status of the project. Or, if they prefer an email instead, offer to send them status updates via email. Make sure you send the status emails directly to them, and don't proxy it through anybody else like the account rep or customer support.

A QUICK RECAP

1. Companies earn money selling products or services, and when they fail, customers get upset, varying by customer type: individual consumers, enterprise customers, and SMBs.

2. SMBs complain the most, as any impact directly affects their bottom line because they lack the redundancies of larger enterprises.

3. Two types of bad news are missed deadlines and explanations for malfunctions. Understanding and empathizing with the customer's pain is key.

4. When delivering bad news to enterprise customers, apologize, own the delay, provide specifics, offer a new delivery date, and maintain transparency and empathy.

CHAPTER 7

How to Deliver Bad News to Customers: System Problems

It was mid-2021, COVID was raging, and I was a CTO at a Southern California–based e-commerce company. I had inherited a set of systems that had extensive stability issues. Thankfully the engineers I inherited were pretty good, so as soon as I joined, I refocused most of them to fix the stability issues.

One of the operational issues I had to deal with was the amount of spam flowing through our systems. Every software company has their share of bad customers who want to subvert the software in malicious ways. One of the core features of our product was the ability to send mass emails, which was probably more loved by the bad actors than our legitimate customers, and they loved to send spam. Spam is annoying to the people who receive it, but to the systems that send that spam, they can be a death knell. If your servers send too much spam, they will start getting blocked by various inbox providers like Gmail, Microsoft, Yahoo, and so on. This means that *all* email sent by your system will be blocked. Which is what happened to us.

We got blocked by Spamhaus, which is a very influential authority when it comes to email reputation. If Spamhaus thinks you are a bad actor, lots of inbox providers will think so as well. Once Spamhaus blocked us, 80 percent of all emails our system was sending were not getting delivered to customers. The email system was a critical component of our customer's workflow, and when it went down, the pitchforks went up.

They were pissed. They yelled at us through all available channels. Social media, customer support, emails, and one customer actually yelled at me on LinkedIn. In the beginning, I was just as frustrated. In my mind, I was wondering why customers didn't understand that yelling at me or my team was just distracting us from solving the issue.

In a moment of impossible serendipity and a bit of madness, I decided to read all the hate mail that I had gotten. I painfully went through a lot of it. Amid the pitchforks was a legitimate question. I realized that the biggest reason they were angry was because they didn't know what the hell was going on and nobody was able to answer their basic questions like, what happened to their emails?

When I looked at the status page, I noticed that it only had one update on it since the incident started. Immediately, I put one person in charge of keeping that page up to date with information. I also brought the support team up to speed with what was going on so that they could answer customer questions when they called the support line. Once regular updates started flowing through to customers, some of the anger died down. However, until the emails started flowing again, the fire wouldn't be put out.

The only way you can get Spamhaus to unblock you is to convince them you are not a wholesale supplier of spam, and the easiest way to do that was to show them that we were blocking spam from going out. Internally, we aggressively started blocking the spam accounts. After three days of aggressively removing bad actors and duct-taping some of the critical holes in the system, Spamhaus removed us from their block list. We were finally able to breathe again. I thought that fixing the issue would herald the lowering of the pitchforks, but I was mistaken. Multiple customers started social media threads calling into question our system's overall reliability and, through proxy, the company's credibility. I decided to address the customers directly via a social media post.

In the post, I first introduced myself to the group, as I was relatively new to the company. It was only fair that the customers knew the name of the person they were yelling at. Then I went into all the gory details about what happened and how we ended up getting blocked by Spamhaus. The truth was, we weren't paying attention to spam for a very long time, with new, sexy, customer-facing features consistently getting prioritized over unsexy spam-blocking initiatives. The sins of the past were what put us in email jail, and I was pretty self-critical about it in my message to the customers. I didn't blame a single person or a team for it; I blamed myself. It doesn't matter who made the wrong decision in your team. In the end, the failures are your own as the leader of the team. Then I went into all the projects we were going to do that would prevent issues like this from happening again. Some of those features would make it harder for customers to send email. We were going to make doubly sure customers would get opt-ins from their customers before sending them emails, which would introduce some additional work for our customers. I laid all of them down as well in my post, making it clear to them that I needed their help to keep the email flowing without disruption.

When I made it clear to customers that I wanted to make them a part of figuring out the solution, the temperature in the community went down considerably. I am not entirely sure if all companies have similar customers, but most customers just want to be included in your thought process. I wonder if most people are like that.

So, to recap, the things that helped me calm my customers down were being self-critical, giving them the details, and including them in designing the fix. Oh, and also some refunds to show the company was willing to lose some short-term profits for a stronger long-term relationship.

Transparency

In Chapter 6, we talk about how to tell your customer that you are not going to deliver on a feature commitment. This chapter explores how to navigate situations when you have a systems problem like your service stops working for your customers, causing disruption. Now, you have to go in front of people and explain to them what happened and convince them to stick around as customers. Fair warning, this chapter is heavily focused on software engineering situations, but these can be adapted for your situation.

The most important thing your customers are looking for is transparency. Yes, they care about the service starting to work again, but they care more about the details of the outage and also about how timely those details are made available to them.

Broadly, there are three things customers want to know: (1) what happened, (2) how the problem affects them, and (3) what you are doing to prevent issues like this from happening again. You need a robust multichannel approach to communicating with customers in the event of service outages. At the minimum, every service company needs the following channels in place to communicate effectively with their customers:

- A web-based status page where your customers can get the overall status of the service they are paying for (e.g., https://health.aws.amazon.com/health/status)

- An internal incident management system that keeps all relevant internal stakeholders (product teams, customer support, customer success, etc.) informed so that they are ready to tackle questions from customers

- An online community where your customer can interact with their service provider (in this case, you and your company) and other customers (e.g., https://support .zendesk.com/hc/en-us/community/topics, https:// aws.amazon.com/developer/community/)

- A mass emailing system (e.g., https://www.mailgun .com/, https://www.twilio.com/)

If you sell to enterprises, you probably also have dedicated account managers for your customers.

A Process for Responding to Service Issues

Let's walk through the process when your service goes down. The first thing to do is to update the status page with the details of the outage. You don't have to put in details if you don't know them, but you have to put something out on the status page to make sure your customers are informed. As your team works through the issue, make sure the status page is up to date. My general guideline to my teams is to update the status page every fifteen minutes. Even if you don't have anything to report besides just saying your team is still working on it, make sure the status page has updates every fifteen minutes. As your team uncovers more details, make sure you update the status page and specifically get into the details of what matters to your end customer. Here is an example from my past:

> Starting at 11/11/2011 at 11am PST, due to a vendor disruption, media encoding in the application may be delayed but functional. If you encounter any issues with a video/file stuck while encoding, you may save the page and try again later. We will update this page as soon as we have more information to share.

Here is an example of all the other status messages associated with the incident. I have removed some of the updates for the sake of brevity.

Identified—Due to a vendor disruption, media encoding in the application may be delayed but functional. If you encounter any issues with a video/file stuck while encoding, you may save the page and try again later. We will update this page as soon as we have more information to share.

Update—The vendor has implemented a fix and antici-pates that encoding queues will be cleared by 7pm PST. We are continuing to monitor for any performance improvements or changes with media encoding services and other queues. If you encounter any issues uploading media, we recommend saving and returning to the page later. Thank you for your patience, and we will post updates to this page as soon as we have more information to share.

Resolved—The incident has been resolved. The vendor has finished processing the backlog of uploaded media.

The common themes across these updates are as follows:

- It is precise about what is not working and what is working.

- It is precise about when the issue started happening.

- It is precise about how the incident affects the end customer and any actions they need to take.

For partial outages (as in the previous case), you don't need to do much beyond regular updates to the status page, and make sure your customers know the URL for the status page.

In the case of full application outages, where everything is down for everyone, or in the event of a security incident (large-scale phishing, accounts compromised, etc.), your managers need to directly address your customers. This is where the pitchforks will be thrown at you.

Once the incident has been resolved, you will need to write a production incident follow-up report. The best way to showcase how to write this follow-up is with an example. This is what I wrote up when our managed redis instance (used for caching) failed, bringing down the entire application for an hour:

> Hey, all! My name is Mahesh, and I run engineering here at Kajabi. First off, I want to deeply apologize for the disruption this incident has caused your business.
>
> I want to share what we know so far about what happened, and what steps we are taking to mitigate future occurrences of this issue.
>
> We have isolated the problem to a vendor product we use for caching application requests. We noticed this morning that caching servers were taking longer than usual to respond to requests. At that point, we engaged with the vendor to help us mitigate the issue. We've taken additional steps (spun up an additional caching server) to reduce response times down to normal levels. We have a few more changes scheduled for later tonight that we expect to protect against this issue. However, we are still investigating what exactly caused the cache cluster to start behaving abnormally in the first place. My team is actively working with the vendor to get to the bottom of this.

Additionally, we are accelerating our efforts (which were already underway) to continue to invest in our infrastructure, including caching (we are strongly considering moving to a new provider), such that we are better supporting and serving your businesses.

I really apologize for the disruption and impact this had on your businesses, and for that I am truly sorry, and I appreciate your patience as we work to get this resolved as quickly as possible.

This message shares a lot of similarities with the status page updates mentioned earlier but is different in one big, meaningful way: It is personal. It shows that I, the leader in charge, personally care about the incident.

In the event of a large-scale system outage that caused tremendous disruption for your customers, the single most important thing they are looking for is transparency. Not just transparency from the company but transparency from an actual person as well. Specifically, they want to see accountability from the person directly responsible for the upkeep of the system they depend on daily. Just owning up to the outage and directly responding to customers will go a long way in earning back trust from them. Whatever industry you are in, strive for transparency and accountability with your customers, and they will, on the whole, respect you for it.

Two-Way Communication

You score even more points of trust if you allow two-way communication with your customers, such as engaging with them on social media and answering questions. Yes, you will get some (and, in some cases, a lot of) hate from your customers in online interactions. I typically don't engage with any sniping that comes my way, but I do engage with customers who are genuinely worried about the future of the service. I won't respond to posts like, "Clearly you are incompetent, and the company needs a new engineering leader." And, yes, that is a real quote that got thrown at me by a customer.

But I do respond to questions like, "There have been several incidents in the past few months, what is going on?" with something like this:

> Hey, X, I apologize for the disruption we caused you. There have been three partial incidents (fixed in under fifteen minutes) and one full application outage (fixed in sixty minutes) in the last six months. There wasn't any common theme across the incidents except human error. To reduce the chance of human errors happening, we have increased our investment in test automation. So far, those errors haven't happened again. I am sure there will be more human-caused production incidents as we ship new features, but we will continue to keep working on creating a good balance between velocity of shipping and quality.

The key is to respond with empathy, data, honesty, and accountability.

If you have VIP customers, just sending an email or engaging with them on social media won't be enough. You will have to get on the phone with them. The script is pretty much the same as the recent example, but you have to personalize this conversation. When you talk to them, you have to showcase that you understand *their* business and the impact your system outage had on their bottom line. Walk them through the details of what caused the incident, why mitigation steps took whatever time they did, and the future road map items that will prevent issues like this from happening again.

A QUICK RECAP

1. Understand your customer and personalize your responses to them.

2. Take ownership and show accountability.

3. Lean into transparency. Don't be afraid to get into the details with your customers.

4. Develop a thick skin.

CHAPTER 8

How to Deliver Bad News to Your Team: Changing to a Better Direction

In a galaxy far, far away, I inherited an engineering team that was growing quickly but was experiencing significant teething pains. The team that was struggling the most was the production engineering team. The concept of production engineering came from Shopify. Production engineering's focus (as developed by Shopify) was supposed to be part developer tools (to make developers more efficient at shipping quality performant code) and part infrastructure operations. At Shopify, the production engineering teams were partially staffed with software developers (to focus on developer tools) and partially staffed with SRE (site reliability engineers).

In my second week at the company, I got a very unusual request from one of the lead engineers in the production engineering team. He wanted an executive assistant to help him out. I stared at the email for quite some time, just to make sure I understood the request correctly. Executive assistants are personal assistants who assist senior leaders with time management, travel, events, and so on. They are typically attached only to executives (C-suite, VPs, etc.), so I was flabbergasted at this request. I was new to the organization, so I didn't want to just immediately scoff at the request and deny it.

Instead, I decided to find out more. The lead engineer replied with a backlog of items he thought an EA could help him with. The items ranged from pending requests from the developers to backlogged requests from the finance team about cost management. All those things seemed legitimate, but what puzzled me was why he and his team were not able to handle that load. The load was definitely on the higher side, but it seemed doable for a team of eight, so I dug in more. After some quick digging, I found the wrench that was jamming up the gears of the team. The root cause was the on-call load. This production engineering team, for some unknown reason, had decided to act as first-level support for the entirety of the engineering organization. This team of eight was responding to any system incident that happened across the application regardless of whether they ever worked on (or owned) that part of the system or not. When I asked why the rest of the engineering team was not stepping in to offset their load, the answer I got was that the rest of the engineering team was uncomfortable going on call because they had never done it before.

Being on call can be stressful. You could get paged in the middle of the night and be expected to fix a system issue that could affect a large swath of your customer base. It requires the engineer to think on their feet and make quick decisions with very little data. When the application is down, there isn't a lot of time to spare. In some cases, your decisions might prove to be incorrect, so the engineer also needs to be comfortable with pivoting quickly. I fully understood why the development team was reluctant to handle the on-call responsibility. However, the pressure cooker situation the production engineering team was in was untenable. I had to make a change quickly before that team decided to rage quit together.

The first thing I wanted to do was to give the team more permanence. I worked with the product team and came up with a team structure that had permanent focus areas. There wasn't too much pushback from anyone about this change, so I got this change through quickly and moved on to the bigger challenge of getting the development team on an on-call rotation to offset the load from the production engineering team. This was going to be tough. Nobody likes it when their cheese is moved, especially if it is moved to a completely new maze setup in a completely different room that is watched over by a strange new creature (the new CTO).

I first broached this change with the people leaders reporting to me. As I talked to them, it became clear that the biggest fear in their teams was the fear of the unknown. "What do I do when I get paged?" "What happens if I sleep through the page?" "What do I do if I need to pull in some other team?" And the biggest fear of all, "What do I do if I don't know how to fix the problem?"

Once I got a sense of what the engineers were afraid of, I put together a rollout plan that addressed most of their concerns. I worked with the production engineering team to come up with a training course that I put all teams through. Then I picked a couple of teams that were moderately enthusiastic about this change and empowered them to lead the charge in terms of coming up with an on-call rotation, runbooks (systematic procedures for achieving desired outcomes), and practice drills. Additionally, I encouraged them to share their learnings with other teams. However, the most important thing that the engineers cared about was the safety net. "Who is going to help if I get stuck? Am I doing this the right way?"

To put my team at ease, I added myself to the on-call rotation for all alerts. This meant I'd get paged if anyone on my team (except the production engineering team, because they already had a rotation going) got paged for anything. I did this for the next three months. Most of the time I only acted as a rubber duck for my engineers. For people who don't know, the act of rubber ducking is to narrate your thought process as you solve a problem to someone else who isn't going to respond with any opinions of their own. Just the act of narrating the problem to someone else will reveal the answer to you.

At the end of the three months, the team was comfortable enough to start handling on-call rotations by themselves. Just showing up along with my team and supporting them in the moment greatly increased my trust and credibility with them. As Patton said, "Always do everything you ask of those you command."[9] Also, it helped me get a crash course on the intricacies of how the system worked, including the friendly gremlins who lived in them. In about six months, on-call rotation became a way of life for my team. Another successful transformation was in the bag.

---

9   Porter B. Williamson, *Patton's Principles* (Tucson, AZ: Management and Systems Consultants, 1979), 19.

Making Your Team Do Something They Dislike

A good manager should aim for bottom-up thinking 99.9 percent of the time. As a leader, you come up with a set of problems that are aligned with your company's goals, and your team comes up with creative ways to solve those problems. Let your team self-organize and find solutions. However, there will be moments when you have to force your team to do something they don't want to.

There are two versions of this. The first is when you have to realign your team in a direction you know they will hate, but you firmly believe in the new direction. For example, you are going to sunset (stop a project midway) a project your team loves to work on; it isn't contributing positively to the bottom line, so you decide to kill it.

The other version of this is when you do not agree that the thing you are going to do is the right thing, and you know your team will dislike it, but you have to do it because your boss (or their boss) has made a corporate decision and you have decided to disagree and commit. Examples would be a mandatory return to the office, bonuses slashed because of macroeconomic conditions, and so forth. In this chapter we focus on the easier of the two, the former.

The third and last version of this is when you have to go back on a promise you made to the team. Examples could be compensation changes you promised but had to walk back because of exogenous changes, promotions you promised but had to walk back, and so on.

Organizing for Clear Communication

The first thing you should do is sit down and organize your thoughts into a structured communication plan. The communication plan should address the following (at the minimum):

1. What is changing?

2. Why is it changing?

3. Why is it changing now?

Here is an example document that I wrote for myself when I decided to decentralize the on-call rotation and spread it across all product development teams:

1. What is changing?

   Starting on mm/dd/yyyy, the Operations Team will not be the first-line responder for paging events generated by our automated system monitors. Instead, the team that owns a specific subsystem will start responding to pages directly. This means that our team will now be directly responsible for responding to paging events 24x7, starting mm/dd/yyyy.

2. Why is it changing?

   The Operations Team owns only a specific part of our system, specifically the hosting infrastructure. They have little knowledge about how various customer-facing features work, and typically, they turn around (introducing delays) and end up calling/

texting/paging the tech lead of the product development team to actually fix the issue. As our systems grow larger and our teams grow correspondingly larger, the only logical solution is to decentralize first-line support. Last, the Operations Team is not incentivized to fix any long-term subsystem issues that the paging events surface, because they don't own those subsystems. The product development teams do.

3. Why is it changing now?

It is changing now because of two things. First, our application footprint has considerably grown both in size and in complexity over the last few years. Second, the production engineering team is getting paged multiple times every day, including nights and weekends. An operationally burdened team that has no means to reduce its paging burden will eventually burn out.

4. How does it affect the daily rhythms of the team?

The engineering managers will work with their teams to come up with an on-call rotation and runbooks for their services. All teams here at [company name] have more than five engineers, so assuming a weekly rotation, most engineers will have to go on-call once a month. The engineering managers will be in the escalation chain; for example, if both the primary and secondary on-call don't respond to the page in fifteen minutes, the system will automatically page their managers. I will be the final node in the escalation chain.

5. Can I opt out of this?

No, everybody in engineering will be part of the on-call process. If you have paid time off scheduled on an on-call week, you can swap slots with somebody else on your team.

6. What does success look like?

The end goal is to increase the overall stability of the systems we manage. Currently, the team who is handling the alerts can't fix the underlying issues that caused the alerts, because they don't own those systems. As a result, the alerts keep occurring and the underlying stability issues don't get fixed. With this change, the team getting paged can fix the issue causing the alerts, which will eventually lead to higher overall stability.

7. Will we prioritize production stability over product development?

In most cases, yes.

Stick to Your Plan

Change is hard. Most adults do not like to be told what to do. Resistance to directives is as old as humanity itself. Most people want to experience life in their own way. Stumbling along, failing, learning, adapting, and eventually evolving into better versions of themselves. Business teams are no different. They want to figure things out on their own. They want to experiment with new technologies, to learn from their mistakes, and to become a better team. So, when a leader gives them a directive, expect resistance. The resistance will come in many forms. The employees will characterize you as an outsider. They will accuse you of being authoritarian. Finally, they will portray you as somebody who is trying to change the culture of the organization. All of those will hurt.

As you roll out these changes, make sure you're available to your teams to answer any questions or concerns they might have. In those conversations with employees, resist the temptation to revisit decisions. There will always be a group of people who will be passionately opposed to any meaningful change. If you have people-pleasing tendencies like me, you might be tempted to go back and change the decision you have made to please those groups of people. Resist it at all costs. Organizational changes take time to show results. You won't know if you made the right decision in a day or two. It will take weeks and months and sometimes even years. Also, going back on your decision will cause whiplash, and soon your team will start feeling that you are not a decisive leader, further deteriorating their trust in you. Listen to everybody's concerns sincerely, but make it clear to everybody that you intend to stick to the decision you have made for at least six months or longer. Give everybody a voice but not a vote.

A QUICK RECAP

1. Not all team changes are democratic in nature.

2. Before communicating changes to your team, write down the following:

   a. What is changing?

   b. Why is it changing?

   c. Why is it changing now?

3. Expect and plan for resistance from your team.

4. Remember that in some situations, everybody gets a voice, not a vote.

CHAPTER 9

How to Deliver Bad News to Your Team: Disagree and Commit

I n a galaxy not so far away, I was an engineering leader managing a small company. The pandemic had just ended. The mask restrictions were on their way out. The company had just hit a hundred million in revenue. We had just wrapped up a full company on-site week, and employee morale was the highest it had been in the past twenty-four months. Life was good, until fate decided to stir some shit up.

CEOs are a mercurial bunch, and this CEO was no different. One day, after walking around the mostly empty office, he decided to bring people back to the office. Okay, fine, I am probably oversimplifying it. I am sure other productivity-related reasons precipitated the grenade the CEO lobbed at the organization.

The CEO decided that everyone within a thirty-mile radius of the headquarters must come into the office at least three days a week. Then it was up to us, the executive team, to push that message down. The plan was to first develop a set of talking points for the people managers, discuss it with the managers, and then finally send out a company-wide email (which would be discussed with the executive team before sending) detailing the change and other FAQs surrounding it. Obviously, the corporate gods decided not to cooperate, and the whole plan exploded like the *Hindenburg*.

Where to start? The email from HR went out *before* the managers got their talking points. As soon as the email hit employee inboxes, the internal Slack channels lit up like the Fourth of July. Employees were filled with confusion, anger, and disbelief. HR made the mistake of trying to explain an unpopular decision with shaky assumptions. A few months ago, we, as a company, got together in person for a week. The goal was to get teams to hang out in person and get to know each other better. Half of the engineering team was hired virtually, so a lot of the engineers met each other for the first time in the on-site. The event was a huge success. The results of the survey that HR did a few days after the on-site clearly showed that the entire employee base loved hanging out in person. HR decided to use the survey results to justify the "return to office" mandate. The gist of the email was, "We believe that you will be happier coming to work because you can then work with your team in person. You all said so yourself in the survey that we sent out after the company on-site."

The employees fell on this misguided message from HR like a pack of wolves and tore it apart. In the internal Slack channel, they repeatedly (and angrily) pointed out that most engineering teams had a mix of local and remote people. In fact, only one team (out of a total of twelve teams) was fully local and would benefit from a physical office. They also painfully pointed out that coming to a once-a-year casual company on-site vastly differed from commuting daily to a physical office and wasting many precious hours in a car. Our HR team tried to put out the fire, but this was a fire that had to burn through its course.

Next, the employees fell on their direct managers. They all demanded answers and explanations from their leaders, who had none. The managers never got their talking points in time. So they pushed their frustrations and anger upward to me. I decided to pull all my angry and frustrated managers into a Zoom meeting. Twelve sets of accusing eyes stared at me in disbelief, anger, and confusion. The tension in the room was thick enough to cut with a butcher knife. I got peppered with all the questions I anticipated: "Why are we doing this? What's the f'in' reason?" "Remote work has been proven to be more effective!" "Do you support this?" "Did you fight hard for us?" and so on.

Before logging into the meeting, I had decided not to try to defend the decision with data. However, in the first five minutes of the meeting, I wavered from my resolve quite a bit. I started off by calling the decision a policy change but then veered off into the unsafe territory of gut feelings. Once I started arguing on the basis of my own personal beliefs (I actually prefer an in-person culture), the meeting started to sour. In the middle of arguing a point, I suddenly remembered my resolve from before and pivoted back to my original message. I kept repeating the fact that I disagreed and committed to the company policy and that I expected them to do the same. After a few more jabs at me, the team resigned themselves to the reality that they had to adapt to a new world where they and their local employees would have to commute to the office. Well, except one. One engineering manager was incredibly incensed about this change. After a few days, he messaged me, asking for a one-on-one meeting.

When I met him over a Zoom call, it was clear that he was still exasperated about the whole thing. For the first ten minutes, he argued against the mandate and tried to change my mind. This was after I had already pointed out to him that the decision couldn't be unmade. After a few more minutes of pointless arguing, he said, "Mahesh, I don't think I can disagree and commit to this decision. It goes against everything I believe in." Now I knew what was going on. He knew that disagreeing and committing to this decision would eat away at his conscience. What I told him next caught him by surprise. I told him that he should leave the company if he couldn't fully disagree and commit. I explained to him that I wasn't asking him to leave because he was defying a company policy but because I knew that if I forced him to comply, his frustration would grow, and, eventually, he would come to distrust the entire executive team, which would frustrate him even further. And then he would leave, completely disillusioned and broken. The manager chose the less painful path and resigned that evening.

Unpopular Decisions

In Chapter 8, we discuss how to roll out changes that you believe are necessary but your team thinks are not. In this chapter, we discuss the strategy to roll out changes you disagree with (gulp). These could be changes your manager is pushing down or that are being pushed down by the executive team. Before we dive in, let's get a bit philosophical.

Being a manager is awesome 99 percent of the time, but this chapter is about the other 1 percent. As a manager, you will be asked to do things you slightly disagree with or straight-up hate. Obviously, this excludes doing anything illegal or unethical for your boss or company. If you think your company is laundering money, by all means go to the police! The truth is, often, people above you will make decisions that you might not like and will expect you to push that down to the team.

On the surface, most companies might seem like they are run by kind, democratic leaders on a noble world-changing quest. Most well-run and admired companies like Amazon, Microsoft, NVIDIA, and Google allow most decisions to be made at the team level and generally give lots of autonomy. However, the cold reality is, most companies are capitalistic institutions run by an oligarchy. And when the oligarchy decides to make a change, everyone else has to fall in line. The bottom line is that even the most employee-friendly companies, from time to time, will ask their middle management to execute plans the rank and file will hate.

The return-to-office policy that companies started instituting after the end of the COVID pandemic is a great example of an unpopular decision that many managers had to force on their employees. Layoffs are another example of unpopular decisions that people managers might have to help execute. So the question to ask yourself is how do you typically respond to directives handed to you? Do you relentlessly argue with the powers that be? Do you give in to your bosses? Or maybe you are somewhere in the middle?

Disagree and Commit

What every manager is expected to do is to disagree and commit. Individual contributors who aspire to be engineering managers have to absolutely master this skill. Amazon famously codified this as a leadership principle that every employee in the company has to live by.[10] As a leader, you are expected to respectfully challenge decisions you disagree with. However, if a decision has been made, you are expected to stop debating it and commit to executing it. You can't begrudgingly commit to it. You have to commit to it wholly. This means you can't complain to everyone that you disagree with the idea once the decision has been made. You can't grumble to people that somebody else is making you do it. You can't tell people your manager pressured you to do this. Each time you complain to your team about situations like these, you are losing a bit of authority in front of your team. You might think that being transparent with your team about your displeasure in pushing down the change will earn you brownie points with them, but your team will see a manager who doesn't have any decision-making powers. The more this happens, the more the team will feel you, as a leader, can't really help them in any way. They'll see you as a lame-duck manager.

---

10   Amazon Jobs, "Leadership Principles," accessed March 11, 2024, https://www.amazon.jobs/content/en/our-workplace/leadership-principles.

What about situations where you really believe that you can't stand behind an unpopular decision made by the powers above you? If you ever find yourself in a situation where you truly, deeply, philosophically disagree with your manager, the only thing you can do is find a different manager. Or a different company. There is no point in trying to get behind a decision that goes against your internal code of ethics, because if you do, it will slowly eat you up inside. The more you try to live with it, the deeper your loathing toward your bosses becomes until one day you will find yourself completely disillusioned about your manager, company, or both. And then you will leave. Both paths lead to a departure. I recommend choosing the road with the least pain and leaving early.

If you have successfully disagreed and committed and are now ready to roll down the changes, the first thing to do is to write a document that describes the change in detail. The questions you need to answer are similar to the ones we discuss in Chapter 8. For reference, here are two of those questions:

1. What is changing?

2. Why is it changing?

The answer to the first question is straightforward. The answers to the second question are where the dragons live. I am fairly certain that most unpopular decisions are almost always pushed down because one or two people at the top believe in them. I would bet a dollar that most unpopular decisions are impulsive, gut decisions made by the executive team and, in many cases, made by the CEO herself and not driven by data or science. Take the return-to-office policies companies rolled out after the pandemic. The majority of research done around this controversial topic indicates that employees *feel* more productive when they are not wasting hours commuting to a physical office and instead are working from the comfort of their homes in shorts or sweatpants with the heat cranked up to their preference.[11] I have never worked in an office building that was set to a comfortable temperature. I swear thermostats in office buildings are mostly for decoration.

Since their commute time is zero, employees have additional time to devote to health- and wellness-related activities like exercising, getting out of the house often, walking the dog, and so on. And most importantly, they can now spend more time with their families. The line managers who directly manage these employees also feel the same. They feel that remote work results in happier and more productive employees. However, executives and middle managers don't share the same level of optimism as their employees about remote work.

In my opinion, executives want people back in the offices because they don't want to invest time and energy into transforming their office culture to a virtual one. Most companies are not cash cows. They live and die by their ability to keep Wall Street well-fed and happy. Wall Street does not give a damn about employee happiness. They care about the quarterly earnings. Given the pressures on the average CEO and executive, the

---

11 Apollo Technical, "Surprising Working from Home Productivity Statistics," February 7, 2024, https://www.apollotechnical.com/working-from-home-productivity-statistics/.

last thing on their mind is to figure out how to build an effective remote culture. So they revert to what they know works: working in a physical office.

So, going back to the second question earlier, how do you answer why it is changing? The mistake leaders typically make here is to cherry-pick publicly available data like surveys, opinion pieces written by other CEOs, and so on, and try to explain the reason. It won't work. Your team is filled with smart people, and they all know how to use Google. For every supportive piece of evidence you can show, they will show hundreds against it. Such is the nature of unpopular decisions. They are typically not backed by science. One can find multiple pieces of evidence strengthening and weakening both sides of the argument. So do not try to explain it with data. When Elon Musk told Tesla employees to come back to the office, he didn't try to explain his decision with data or science. He just told the employees to come back or quit.[12]

The right way to position an unpopular top-down decision is to position it as a company policy change. When you announce this to employees, I recommend not spending more than thirty minutes on this topic. Invariably, someone (or all) on your team will ask for the supporting evidence behind the policy change. The modern product development team is typically pretty data-driven, and they will poke and prod at the policy change. Be steadfast and do not try to explain the policy

---

12 Jessica Bursztynsky, "Elon Musk Tells Tesla Workers to Return to the Office Full-Time or Resign," CNBC, June 1, 2022, https://www.cnbc.com/2022/06/01/elon-musk-reportedly-tells-tesla-workers-to-be-in-office-full-time-or-resign.html.

change. Also, at some point in the conversation, someone will ask you if you personally believe in the decision. This is where the Kraken sleeps.

Your team will want to know if you support their well-being and happiness or if you are just a corporate acolyte. They will want you to take a side. You can't. Most inexperienced leaders make the mistake of saying, "I really don't want to do this, but the company is forcing me to do it." As I mentioned before, you can't use that line unless you are willing to sacrifice your authority with the team, and you will lose your credibility with your bosses. It is okay to say that you disagreed with this and debated with your higher-ups but have decided to disagree and commit to this path forward. Focus more on the commit than the disagree.

I am sure after the team meeting, employees on your team would want a one-on-one sit-down with you. They will most likely ask you variations of the same question they asked you in the team meeting. "Are you really supportive of this?" "There is no rationale behind this decision!" "Do you *really* support this?" "Why didn't you fight hard for us?" and so on. Be consistent in your answers. You can't deviate from what you have publicly said. Emphasize the fact that you have decided to disagree and commit to this path forward.

Last, the question of exceptions will come up. Some employees would want exceptions. Think carefully before approving exceptions to the policy. When my company announced its own return-to-office mandate, I made exceptions for a small group of employees who had either medical conditions or poor childcare coverage that prevented them from coming into the office.

A QUICK RECAP

1. If you want to climb the corporate managerial ladder, be prepared to enforce unpopular top-down mandates.

2. Learn how to disagree and commit. Commit wholly, not begrudgingly.

3. If disagreeing and committing means killing a part of your soul, don't do it. Instead, leave the company.

CHAPTER 10

How to Deliver Bad News to Your Team: Going Back on a Promise

A long time ago, or maybe not so long ago, I was running engineering for an e-commerce company. The company's founder never intended to build a multibillion-dollar company. From the beginning, he only wanted a lifestyle business that would pay the bills for himself and the employees and keep the size of the company small. For about ten years, the company was bootstrapped and never took in any internal investment, just so that they could stay in complete control and never worry about valuations or funding rounds or opinionated Silicon Valley types. Unlike in traditional venture capital–funded companies, which lean on equity compensation quite a bit to attract top talent, this company's employees didn't have any ownership in the company. They had a salary and a bonus, but no stocks or options. The entirety of the company was owned by the founder.

All of this was perfectly normal for a bootstrapped company. And then COVID happened.

During the height of the pandemic, two things happened. One, online commerce exploded in unimaginable ways. People now suddenly stuck inside their house just spent all their money online. My company benefited from the sudden spike in online e-commerce activity tremendously. The year-over-year growth of customers and revenue was breathtaking. The founder decided to capitalize on that moment and put the company on a more traditional high-growth late-stage level.

The company raised external capital (very easily) and also decided to hire a lot more people to expand the business. In high-tech companies, you can't hire top talent if you are unwilling to give them an equity stake in the business. Additionally, the existing employees were also getting increasingly disgruntled about not having an equity stake in the company. There was also growing concern about the company's best employees being poached by competitors and other software companies that were willing to offer stocks or options. After some pushing by me and my executive peers, the company collectively agreed to give out equity to all full-time employees. Everybody was excited, but they also wanted to know when the actual rollout would occur and how much their equity take would be so that they could compare it to other offers in the market and decide next steps.

The actual rollout was dependent on the corporate structure of the company changing, so I couldn't commit to any timelines to my team. However, I got commitment from the executive team about sharing the approximate equity dollar amounts (and future growth projections) with the employees so that it gave them a reference point to compare against the rest of the industry. I expected everyone in my team to act like owners and never say, "It's not my job," and now that every employee was actually becoming an owner (however small it might have been), it made my job as a leader dramatically easier. All of this was received with a lot of enthusiasm and fanfare by my team. I just had one tiny problem. Remember how I mentioned I had commitment from the executive team about sharing rough numbers? Well, it turned out, I didn't.

Only half the executive team thought they were going to share some numbers with employees, and the other half, which included the CEO, didn't think we committed to anything. We were all unreliable narrators. More importantly, our general counsel basically said we couldn't make any half-baked promises like that, and in hindsight, sharing approximate numbers was exactly that. A half-baked half measure. So now, I had to go tell my team that I wouldn't be able to give them what they had been waiting over a year to get. I had to go back on my word.

I jumped on a Zoom call with all the engineering leaders and decided to break the news to them. I apologized to them directly and took responsibility for my failure. With a quavering voice, I said something along the lines of, "I know I promised you this, and I know how long you all have been waiting for this, but unfortunately, I can't give you what you want. I am extremely sorry for going back on my word." Note that I used "I" in the apology. I never said "we" or "the company" or "the executive team" and so on. I didn't blame any other unreliable narrator.

The arrows and pitchforks came fast and furious. The consistent arrow thrown at me was, "This will further erode our trust in you." My consistent answer to that was, "Yes, I understand it. I hope I can earn some of that back when equity does officially get rolled out, which I am still committed to doing next year. I just want to be transparent with all of you about what is going on, even if being transparent means you will lose some trust in me."

Toward the final minutes of that meeting, the arrows finally died out. Everybody's arms were tired of holding the pitchforks up. The group had moved on to acceptance. After the call, a few people reached out to me and empathized with the predicament I was in and expressed some support. Surprisingly (or maybe unsurprisingly), everybody who reached out to me thanked me for my transparency.

Equity rolled out the following year, and everybody lived happily ever after. I think.

Breaking a Promise

This is the final (and possibly the trickiest) type of bad news you might have to deliver to your team. This is when you must go back on your word. Break a promise. Line and midlevel managers are put in this unfortunate situation of breaking their promise for many reasons. However, two of the most common reasons are that the manager prematurely made a promise to their team without getting the blessing of their bosses or their bosses above them went back on their word. Both situations end up putting the manager in a situation where they have to go back to their team and break a promise to them. Yes, this is about how to recant gracefully without losing complete trust with your team, or maybe with losing minimal trust.

Promises work brilliantly when you can honor them. Unfortunately, breaking a promise drains your team's trust battery more than fulfilling them. This is why managers should be extremely careful in making promises. In general, my advice to managers is to not make promises about outcomes. I have a pessimistic view about permanence in corporations, so I recommend that managers commit to the path but not the outcomes. However, if you are truly committed to the path and put in the work, there is a decent chance that you will achieve the outcome you were working toward. The only time a promise is probably appropriate is when your team's trust battery is close to zero and there is only an upside to promising something to your team.

But if you do get to a point when you have to break a promise you made to your team, there are a few things you can do to salvage your reputation. A lot of what I say in Chapters 6 and 7, when discussing how to deliver bad news to customers, is applicable here as well. When you meet with your team, you have to focus on three broad things: the apology, what happened, and the follow-up.

The Apology

When you meet your team (in person, if possible) to deliver the news of the broken promise, start off with an apology. Don't try to deflect blame on the unreliable narrators in the company. Your team has to collectively hear you say the words "I am sorry, but I can't give you what I promised," not "We are sorry," or "The company is sorry," or "The leadership team is sorry." The only thing that will do is "I am sorry." Say it with humility and say it like you mean it.

Empathy and vulnerability have been recognized as markers for leadership excellence for at least a couple of decades,[13] if not more. However, even in this day and age, leaders struggle to apologize authentically in public. In my opinion, this is partially due to the rise of the Silicon Valley "tech bro" CEO. Tech bro CEOs tend to hire tech bro executives. I also think there are a lot of CEOs and executives who are in their seats not because they're the most qualified for those jobs but because they aggressively lobbied for it or just asked for it. Or it could simply be that the world still leans toward hiring type A, brash, aggressive extroverts as executives, even though research says empathetic leaders perform better.

Regardless of what your personality type is, you have to learn to apologize authentically in public. A lot of literature is out there about how to apologize,[14] but I will mention one easy technique you can use to deliver a sincere apology. Leave out the "but." "I apologize for this, but . . ." followed by many sentences that deflect blame away from you. For example, "I apologize for

---

13 Tracy Brower, "Empathy Is the Most Important Leadership Skill According to Research," *Forbes*, September 19, 2021, https://www.forbes.com/sites/tracybrower/2021/09/19/empathy-is-the-most-important-leadership-skill-according-to-research/?sh=1170ac633dc5.

14 Brett Beasley, "How the Best Apologies Are Made," Notre Dame Deloitte Center for Ethical Leadership, accessed March 14, 2024, https://ethicalleadership.nd.edu/news/how-the-best-apologies-are-made/. Also see Barbara Kellerman, "When Should a Leader Apologize—and When Not?," *Harvard Business Review*, April 1, 2006, https://hbr.org/2006/04/when-should-a-leader-apologize-and-when-not.

this, but the real issue is with the marketing team." Replace that with, "I apologize for this. This is my mistake, and I am sorry. I know I have lost trust with you all, so I am going to work on making myself better and making sure this communication mishap with the marketing team doesn't happen again."

Another easy way to get better at expressing authentic contrition is by freely apologizing to people who are lower in the societal or corporate hierarchy compared to you. I never hesitate to apologize to interns, my team, other teams, customers, and the cleaning crew who would come in at 6:00 p.m. to clean the office. Especially if I am holding them up.

I also apologize to my son freely. There is nothing more humbling than looking at a smaller version of you who is looking up at you with disappointment, tear-filled eyes, and quivering lips, and saying, "I am sorry for getting upset at you." There is also nothing more rewarding than your son hugging you as an acceptance of your apology. I doubt your teams will forgive you that easily, but I digress.

What Happened

Once you are done with your apology, get into a little bit of detail around "what happened." Describe the path you went through and the moment when the stairs turned Escheresque[15] and the gold turned to coal. It is okay to point blame on a failed process

---

[15] For examples of M. C. Escher's works, see https://mcescher.com/gallery /impossible-constructions/.

or poor communication, but it is not okay to point blame on any individual besides yourself.

After you have described how the process malfunctioned, talk about how you are going to fix it going forward. Last, leave plenty of time for questions and bear any additional lashes your team wants to give you. However, if at least one individual reaches out after the meeting and expresses sympathy for your situation, you just might have survived the debacle with at least a tiny bit of trust still left in the battery.

The Follow-Up

Give your team about a week to process the bad news you gave them and then follow up with them. Your goal is to assess how much trust you have left with your team. If you hear variations of "I was disappointed, but I understand how things came to be," you are probably okay. But if you hear variations of "I am disappointed, and I am not sure I can trust the decisions of this company," you are probably looking at some fallout in the form of attrition. After your final follow-up, don't discuss the details of the past unless you absolutely have to. No point in tearing open recently healed wounds.

A QUICK RECAP

1. Don't make promises to your team unless you really need to.

2. Commit to the path versus outcomes.

3. Companies are filled with unreliable narrators. Expect miscommunications to occur.

4. If you have to go back on your promise, take personal responsibility and apologize authentically.

5. Practice apologizing to your child.

CHAPTER 11

How to Deliver Bad News to Your Boss

I remember the time I had a boss who was a bona fide enigma. His credentials were impressive, but it didn't show in the way he interacted with his organization of more than four hundred people. He didn't talk much, and when he did open his mouth in meetings, it was almost always a piece of blunt criticism. He rarely thanked anybody in public. He was pretty much inactive on common Slack channels and never engaged with any popular watercooler threads. Nobody knew anything about his personal life because he never shared it with anyone. Nobody in the company knew what made him tick, what made him angry, what made him laugh, or what he cared about. As I said, a bona fide enigma. And then there was his facial expression.

He didn't have one. Actually, he did have one, but no one could infer anything from it. He showed no emotion on his face. No raised brows, no frowns, no smiles, no nothing. No one could tell what he was thinking or how he was feeling. His face looked as if it were carved in stone. Nothing moved. The expression he wore on his face was not dissimilar to the one worn by the farmer in the famous painting *American Gothic*. If I have to pick one word to describe his resting facial expression, it would be "puritanical." As a lifelong learner and user of facial expressions, I was immensely frustrated. And not just I but everyone in the company was utterly baffled by the demeanor of this new enigmatic leader.

A few months after he was hired, he started to make meaningful changes to the way the business was run, which in turn started affecting employee workflows. Because he was emotionally unavailable, employees were reluctant to give him any direct feedback. The one or two times people tried to give him feedback, they were met with mostly indifference. As a result, most employees resigned themselves to begrudgingly carry out his bidding, including myself. He was our boss after all. Until one day I decided to change that.

The disaster that precipitated my change in attitude was the departure of a key member of my team. One of my teams was working on a project deemed critical by our mysterious overlord. As a result, the team worked nights and weekends to get this project over the finish line just to make the boss happy. I was trying my best to keep their spirits up, but the obvious lack of validation from the uber boss was not lost on the team.

The project's lead engineer was the most burnt out. The lead engineer was a very empathetic leader who was very much in sync with his team's emotions and cared tremendously about their work-life balance. So, when the team started to work nights and weekends to hit the deadline, he decided to work even harder, to give the rest of his team some relaxation over the weekends. After a couple of months of him burning the midnight oil, his wife stepped in and reminded him that if he kept working at this pace, he was going to have a heart attack. He spent days deliberating about the project, the company, and his leaders before he decided to quit and put in his notice. I got on a call with him and tried to convince him to stay, but it was clear from the beginning that he had made up his mind. He was also not the mudslinging type, so he tried to keep his true reasons for leaving private, but when I kept pressing, he finally gave me the real reason. He said, "Mahesh, you are a terrific leader. You are not the reason I am leaving. I am leaving because your boss is extremely uninspiring. I can't follow someone who has the personality of a fish."

I was speechless. I was stunned. But not surprised. At this point the new leader had been in the company for close to a year, so I was pretty sure most of the organization knew about his personality or lack thereof. So I wasn't surprised that this lead engineer had caught on to the new leader's *American Gothic* persona. What stunned me was that an engineer who'd been three levels removed from this new leader and had probably one interaction with him in his time at the company was leaving a stable organization with really good compensation and a team that he really loved just because the boss's boss was lacking personality. In the end, I just told the engineer he was making the right decision. Life is too short to be spent following poor leaders.

Until then, I had never given any adaptive feedback to any of my bosses. I had never told any past boss that they were not inspirational enough. This time around, I decided to change that. I wasn't sure if my current boss would change and suddenly start engaging with his teams more, but I was sure delivering that feedback would unlatch the iron maiden that had started to clamp down on my conscience since the day my new boss got hired.

I reached out to a handful of peers and mentors about how to give adaptive feedback, but I didn't get anything useful besides almost everyone wishing me good luck. Gulp. So I wrote down a few tenets for myself before getting on the call with my boss:

- I will be kind.

- I won't expect any change to happen.

- I won't mince words or soften the message.

- I will be ready to part ways with the company if needed.

The last one was pretty important because it acted as the ultimate release valve for me. What was the worst that could happen? They might fire me, and that was okay by me. So I decided to drop the feedback on him in our next one-on-one. The exact words I wanted him to hear were, "Bob left because he thinks you are not inspirational, and others might leave if you don't change that perception of yours."

He was a few minutes late, and by the time he joined the call, I was a nervous wreck. My palms were sweaty even though I had stuffed them into my front pockets because the office thermostat was set to freezing. My heartbeat was so loud that it was reverberating all the way up to my temples. After joining the call, he fixed his perpetually disappointed dad stare at me and said, "What's up?" At that moment, I almost lost my nerve and decided not to share what was on my mind. Almost. But then I thought about the iron maiden of shame and guilt tightening around my conscience, and I decided to go through with it.

I started off by saying, "Hey, as you know Bob is leaving, and when I tried to save him, he told me that he is leaving because he doesn't find you inspirational." My boss leaned forward and said, "Hmm, okay." But his demeanor slightly changed. His eyes took on a look of curiosity. He wanted to know more! That was my cue to continue speaking, so I took it and ran with it.

I gave him my point of view on how leaders should engage with their teams. How and when to be empathetic. How to act in crisis moments without eroding trust. How using fear to motivate teams does not work, and so on. I ended my impromptu leadership sermon with a warning. If he couldn't figure out how to craft and share an inspirational vision, more good people would leave. Throughout my spiel his impassive demeanor didn't change much. He didn't ask any questions, interrupt me, or defend his actions. When our time ran out, he just hung up after saying a quick goodbye.

I felt relieved. My conscience had successfully broken out of the iron maiden of guilt. I was slightly fearful for my future in the company, but the overwhelming sense of deliverance smothered every other emotion that tried to rise to the surface.

What happened to the taciturn leader? Not much. However, a few weeks after our conversation, I did get a Slack message from him thanking me for an all-nighter I had pulled the day before to put out a crisis. That was the very first time I had received any Slack message from him that wasn't a question or a complaint. A small win. I would take it.

Technical and Adaptive Feedback

First, let's clear up a common misunderstanding. It is fashionable for the current crop of leaders (including executive ones) to say that they are totally open to feedback. It is mostly false. From my experience, the more senior the person, the less they will be open to feedback. That is the harsh truth.

In the book *Leadership on the Line*, the authors talk about two types of issues that leaders face: technical issues and adaptive issues.[16] Technical issues have known solutions. For example, if you see a spike in production incidents, you can fix it by allocating more people toward stabilizing production. Adaptive issues require changing people's hearts and minds. If most leaders in your organization are assholes, fixing that will take an overhaul of the company's belief systems, which will require people's hearts and minds to change.

I believe feedback also comes in two flavors. Technical feedback and adaptive feedback. If you want your manager to reduce the number of meetings, they will make it happen. It is technical feedback with a known solution. However, if you want

---

16 Ronald A. Heifetz and Marty Linsky, *Leadership on the Line: Staying Alive through the Dangers of Change*, rev. ed. (Boston: Harvard Business Review Press, 2017).

them to change their attitude, it is almost impossible, because it requires changing their heart and mind, which is an adaptive change and near impossible to do for most people.

In my opinion, the people most walled off to adaptive feedback are people with C titles. It makes sense though. Companies hire C-level leaders in specific roles because they have a specific skill set and a specific way of operating. If they are infinitely pliable and malleable through feedback, they will most likely not be able to accomplish what they were hired to do. A cost-cutting CEO is expected to cut costs ruthlessly and not suddenly become empathetic to the organization's feelings because of feedback they got from their organization. I also believe (maybe to a lesser extent) that as they grow older, they become set in their ways. Why change the very thing that brought you success in your career?

If giving feedback is filled with so much peril, why even bother? Because it is good for your soul. I know it sounds cheesy, but I believe it is true. If something is weighing heavily on your mind, you have to do something to get rid of that baggage. The common trap people fall into is airing their grievances to a peer or a friend. They complain about their bosses to their friends. That won't lighten your load. In fact, it will make it even heavier. The longer you go without acting on it, the more frustrated you will become, and one day you will realize that you have become ineffective in your job. Earlier in my career, when I used to withhold feedback, it started to affect my personal life as well. I used to get annoyed at my family for no reason. Withholding feedback is like holding your breath. You can only go so long without exhaling.

Deciding Feedback Type

Before you decide to give any feedback to your bosses, figure out if the feedback you are about to give is technical or adaptive in nature. Table 2 shows some examples of adaptive and technical feedback.

All critical feedback should be given in person or on a live video call. Do not put it in an email or on Slack or any form of instant messaging. Emails, Slack messages, and DMs can't properly convey the tone and the emotion behind your feedback. The person receiving the feedback should be able to clearly understand the emotion you are feeling. You need to be able to look into the eyes of the person receiving your feedback and express your sincerity. When giving critical feedback, don't aim for anger, sadness, or grief; instead, aim for genuineness.

If you are giving technical feedback, then the path is pretty clear. Meet your boss in person or on a live Zoom call and give

Table 2. Adaptive and technical feedback

Feedback	Adaptive	Technical
You are not inspirational enough.	X	
You are not giving me enough autonomy.		X
Your team doesn't like you.	X	
You are rude.	X	
You undermined me in public.		X
Your vision for the team is not clear.	X	
How do I solve this problem?		X
I don't have a clear career path.		X
I am not happy with my compensation.		X

the feedback to them. If you already have a solution in mind, suggest it to them when you talk to them. There is no guarantee that they will accept your solution, but bringing a problem and a solution (or multiple when applicable) is always good form. If you are about to give adaptive feedback, you need to strategize a bit first.

Often, adaptive feedback is the harshest type of feedback a person can receive. It will strike a blow at the very foundations of how a person's professional, moral, and ethical compass works. I have yet to meet a person who wasn't shaken in some way after receiving adaptive feedback. Before deciding to give adaptive feedback, you will have to get some sense of how open the other person is to receiving adaptive feedback and also some idea of how they will react. The best way to do that is to give them smaller pieces of adaptive feedback and see how they receive it and what they do about it.

The trick is to use your adverbs intelligently. Take these two sentences, for example:

"That was harsh."

"That was a little harsh."

Adverbs of degree, when used strategically, will dramatically lessen the impact of adaptive feedback, and will allow the receiver to process it without getting overwhelmed by the typical bitterness caused by unfiltered, critical adaptive feedback. As you give lower temperature feedback to the other person, watch for their reactions to determine how they will react to stronger feedback in the future.

If their reaction to watered-down micro-feedback is unintentional unawareness, this person may lack emotional intelligence, for example, and then they are most likely to receive adaptive feedback without blowing up. However, if their reaction is defensiveness, delusions of discipline (i.e., they believe it's their job to be harsh), feigned unawareness, or straight-up rudeness, you can expect that their reaction to stronger adaptive feedback will be poor. To get a complete picture of how your boss will react to stronger feedback, you will have to analyze their reactions to multiple pieces of micro-feedback.

But why put in all this effort? Because a poor reaction to adaptive feedback from your manager can put your relationship with them on notice and jeopardize your career in that company.

Giving adaptive feedback to a new manager is like learning to run for the first time. The first time you decide to run, you probably won't make it more than thirty yards before bending over and trying to catch your breath. But if you do it over and over, and regularly keep increasing the distance you cover, you will begin to master it. A mile becomes two, and two miles becomes five, and soon you will be upgrading your plain trainers for tempo shoes.

Every time I get a new manager, I make it a point to deeply understand what makes them tick. As part of my profile-building exercise, I consistently give them adaptive micro-feedback and see how they react to it. Sometimes I don't even present my thoughts as feedback for them but just as observations. For example, if I just saw them heavily criticizing somebody in a meeting, I might say something like, "That meeting was rough," and see how they react to it. In another part of my profile-building exercise, I watch them carry themselves in both low-pressure and high-pressure situations. One can learn a lot about a person by just observing their body language. Leaning back versus leaning forward conveys a ton of information about how the person feels about you. Leaning forward shows interest, and leaning backward expresses indifference.

In most cases, softer, consistent, adaptive feedback will help you build a fairly robust relationship with your manager. In about six months, you should feel comfortable in starting to give stronger adaptive feedback. As I mentioned before, there is no guarantee that your boss will act on that feedback immediately, but you should do it anyway for the sake of your sanity. However, I have seen some leaders adjust their professional compasses ever so slightly, if they have received the same feedback from multiple employees and peers.

What about situations when you know for a fact that your manager will react to your feedback poorly? Should you bother giving your manager harsher feedback when they didn't react appropriately to softer feedback in the past? The answer is yes, you should still unload that feedback, but you should also be ready to walk away from that job. There have been situations in my career when I was proven wrong and my manager reacted pretty positively to harsh adaptive feedback, but as a rule, when I decide to give harsh upward feedback, I also mentally prepare myself to walk away from that job if my boss decides to make my life miserable. The bottom line is, if your manager consistently reacts negatively to feedback or deflects and ignores your feedback, it is time to move on.

A QUICK RECAP

1. Openness to feedback diminishes with seniority.

2. Feedback comes in two flavors: technical and adaptive.

3. Before giving feedback, decide what type of feedback it is.

4. Adaptive feedback is hard to give, but not giving it will make you feel worse.

CHAPTER 12

How to Deliver Bad News to Defend Good People

A long time ago, I was a midlevel executive in a large-size technology company that was fully enjoying the flowing capital of the 0 percent interest rates and quickly expanding in a different location. I was responsible for building up that site from scratch. Essentially, it involved a lot of hiring.

One of the interesting things about my role was that I was a single-threaded owner, which meant I managed both product and engineering functions, so I was responsible for hiring product and engineering leaders. In those early days of hiring, I hired a product leader whom I would put in my top ten list of product managers I have worked with in my career. They are in the top ten not because of raw product management skills, but because they brought above-average product management skills and top-notch people skills. They were popular with every team and every engineer they worked with, including the most curmudgeonly engineers on my team. Their popularity extended beyond the boundaries of my team, and most people in the company had an easy time working with them. Well, almost everyone.

One engineering leader had some sort of beef with this product manager. I never actually found out why, but whatever the reason, the problem was strong enough to push that engineering leader to complain about my star hire to me and others, but mostly to me. They peppered me with vague narratives about how my star hire was messing everything up for themselves, for their team, and through their actions, painting their leader (yours truly) in a negative light.

I initially ignored it (big mistake), but then the narrative started picking up steam, and soon others in the company, including my direct manager, started asking questions about this employee's competency. So I decided to confront the provocateur directly.

I got on a call with this engineering leader and started digging into their reasons behind putting down this seemingly competent product manager. All I could get from them was weak platitudes about the product manager having a "bad attitude," and when I pressed for more details, I didn't get anything substantial. I was now mostly convinced that there was nothing wrong with this product manager.

I then reached out to all the people (including going all the way to the C-suite) the product manager worked with on a regular basis and asked them for feedback. They all said mostly positive things or a bit of constructive criticism. I was now fully convinced that there was nothing wrong with this product manager.

I wrote up my observations, including making it clear that I was standing behind this product manager and their competency, and I sent it to HR and my manager, and the engineering leader. After a lengthy discussion with HR and my manager, they all reached the same conclusion I landed on. The provocateur got their hand slapped, and the product manager still works for the same company.

At another time, in my position at a different, midsize technology company, shortly after I got hired, I decided to bring on board a very senior engineer from my network as a principal engineer. This way, I could focus on upleveling the managers and the talent management processes, shoring up the product development road map, and ensuring the organization structure scaled with the company. And the principal engineer could focus on upleveling the engineering skills of the engineers in the company, solidifying the technical design review process, and mentoring the engineers with their careers. I had no intention of hiring another principal engineer, so my goal was to give this person a lot of scope and autonomy.

I have very rarely met extremely smart individuals who are not quirky in a noticeable way. This principal engineer (PE) was no different. He was logic-driven all the way and had very little patience with people who argued on the basis of anything besides logic. When he lost his patience, he was in people's faces and would quickly make them uncomfortable. However, he also cared about the emotional well-being of the engineers in the company and spent quite a bit of time helping them navigate career, work, and sometimes even personal challenges. As a result, I got an equal number of complaints and praises about him from the company. But the one thing I was sure about was that he truly cared about the success of the company and the people in it, so I provided cover for him whenever pockets of the company raised their pitchforks at him.

One of the things he deeply cared about was diversity inside the engineering team. Software engineering is still a male-dominated (specifically White and Asian men) industry, and my team wasn't any exception. One way to increase diversity in organizations is to remove bias from the hiring process, and this PE wanted to change the hiring process to be more inclusive. In his proposal, he outlined many changes, including one that almost cratered his career at the company. He posited that a nondiverse interviewing panel would keep hiring nondiverse individuals, so he proposed changing all future interviewing panels to require a person of color, a woman, and a member of the LGBTQ community. When the engineering leadership team (me and my direct reports) and HR leadership reviewed the proposal, it felt right. Taking a stronger stance (requiring diversity in the interviewing panels) would move us in the right direction, so we greenlit the changes. None of us realized that we were holding a neutron bomb that was about to go off spectacularly with the PE catching most of the blast with his face.

The PE got the engineering team together every week to exchange ideas, discuss issues coming in the way of productivity and how to solve them, and so on. He casually shared his proposal with the broader engineering organization in that forum. Everything was going fine until he got to the part about requiring a woman, a person of color, and a member of the LGBTQ community in all interviewing panels. The backlash was severe and swift.

The first issue that the group raised was that the diversity requirements were not discussed with the people (women and Black and LGBTQ folks) who were now required to be part of *all* interview panels. There were only a handful of women and a couple of Black and LGBTQ folks in the company. This meant that they would be part of *all* the interviewing that would happen in the company for the foreseeable future. That was a major time commitment (on top of the regular project work they were assigned), and this was the first they had heard about it.

The second, bigger issue they raised was tokenism. The few diverse folks in the engineering organization rightfully pointed out that making the hiring panels diverse was largely a symbolic, meaningless gesture that wouldn't change much in terms of diversity in the engineering organization, and instead it would overburden the tiny group of diverse individuals in the team. They wanted to see changes at the top of the recruiting funnel. They wanted us to source candidates from much more diverse channels. They wanted us to hire from historically Black colleges. They wanted us to hire more from coding schools, which typically had more diversity than a traditional engineering school. In short, they were furious. The PE was thoroughly embarrassed and ended the meeting by saying, "If I speak more, I will make this worse, so I am ending this meeting. Sorry."

I heard all this secondhand, as I missed that meeting because of a conflict. I jumped on a call with the PE to get the full details. His usual confident, imposing demeanor was gone.

He had his fingers interlaced tightly before him and anxiously rubbed his palms against each other. He was avoiding eye contact with the camera and instead was nervously gazing away. He explained what happened in quick bursts of anxious energy. Interspersed throughout his distressed narration were numerous lamentations of, "I fucked up."

I told him that, yes, he did mess up. I told him that his only mistake was not getting feedback about his proposal from a diverse group of engineers earlier in the project. I also told him he wasn't a racist, probably answering a question he was asking himself in his overheated head. I reassured and reminded him that his intentions were noble. I also pointed out to him that the leadership and HR team had greenlit those changes and were equally responsible for the misstep. Last, I told him that I had his back.

But sadly, it didn't help. He was spiraling down into a deep pit of self-doubt and despair. I knew he would be unproductive if he went back to work. I told him to take a couple of weeks off to recover from the blow to his psyche. He immediately accepted. But before he logged off for two weeks, I told him to write up an apology and post it in the engineering Slack channel where the entire organization congregated, which he did. I also told him to personally reach out to the people who called out his flaws and apologize. Which he also did.

Then I personally reached out to the folks who raised concerns about the proposed hiring plan and individually apologized to them. We spent quite a bit of time discussing the personal intent of the principal engineer who designed the plan. A few of their initial reactions were to label the principal engineer a closeted racist, which I knew was completely off base. Some of them wanted this principal engineer fired immediately. Some of them wanted me fired because I was defending him. I walked them through the entire episode in detail, including how it started with the principal engineer passionately arguing for building a diverse engineering team and its benefits. I reminded them about the instances where he personally helped with a project or helped them out with work-related conflicts. Last, I also personally vouched for him. I repeated this exercise with multiple employees (including the CEO) for many weeks until people's minds started to change. It was a grueling mental exercise, but I knew that if I didn't defend him, nobody would. In the end, everybody agreed that the principal engineer's intentions were good, but the execution was flawed.

The people on your team are your most valuable asset. It is your job as a manager to take care of them through the good times and the bad. Especially the bad.

When You Should Not Disagree and Commit

In previous chapters, we talk about how to disagree and commit. Disagreeing and committing is a critical skill for any leader to have, but disagreeing and committing to every debate is a surefire way to lose trust with your team. There are a few situations when you should lay yourself down on the track. I believe there are generally two worthwhile situations in which you need to push back and not disagree and commit: (1) when people outside your team label someone on your team (or your entire team) as a poor performer and you disagree, and (2) when individuals or teams are making significant invest-ment decisions that are not beneficial to the company and the customers it is serving (discussed in the next chapter). Let's unpack the former now.

Defending People

To defend your team's (or individuals on those teams) perfor-mance, you need to know how they are doing on an ongoing basis. There are three questions you need to be able to answer definitively for every team member: (1) Are they getting their stuff done on time and with high quality (i.e., functional com-petency)? (2) Can they do that without burning bridges with the rest of their team and the organization (i.e., cultural com-petency)? (3) Will they be able to elevate and evolve their capabilities as your organization evolves (i.e., growth compe-tency)? Keep a living document that tracks the progress of every employee against these three dimensions. A document like that is often called an individual development plan, and there are lots of templates available online that you can repurpose for your needs.

The bottom line is that you have to be sure the people on your team are moving the company in the right direction because, at some point, someone will question your team's competency. You need to be prepared to answer it authoritatively. A provocative question that I sometimes ask my leaders when they are unsure of an individual's performance is, "If you can hire somebody else in their place instantly, no questions asked, would you do it?" A software development engineer costs about $500,000 annually, with all benefits included. You need to make sure you can justify the cost.

I encourage managers to reflect on their team's performance every month. I run a monthly talent review where all the managers in my organization get together and collectively reflect and refine our opinion of the engineering team's performance. I use a set of prompts to guide the conversation. Who is doing well and might be ready for a promotion soon? Who is not doing well and needs help? The answer to the first question will showcase how well individuals are growing in a team (growth competency), and the answer to the second question is obviously to talk about the poor performers. The only time a "no" is acceptable as an answer is if the team is newly formed (less than six months old). Otherwise, it indicates that the manager is not paying attention to the performance of their team. Left unattended, mediocrity will almost always slip into the miasma of nonperformance.

I encourage all the managers in the meeting to dig into each other's team performance collectively. The goal is not to create strife but instead to set a high bar for talent by focusing on and nurturing talent. To make sure the managers are focusing on breaking the right boulders, I start every talent review with a public service announcement that goes something like this:

The primary goal of this meeting is to elevate the talent bar for our teams continuously. We will be discussing very sensitive topics about the individuals on our team. Please remember that these are real people with dreams,

aspirations, families, and emotions. So please be respect-
ful and helpful. We are here to help our people. Last,
everything we discuss here should not be shared outside.
Gossiping about our people is a fireable offense. However,
managers should take the feedback they gather here about
their teams and share it with their teams without nam-
ing the individuals who gave the feedback.

If you continuously benchmark your team against the other
teams in the organization and have up-to-date individual development plans, then you will have all the evidence you need to
justify your team's performance.

Critical comments about your team are often off-the-cuff
comments. A seemingly nonthreatening dig at someone on your
team. A gentle jab. "I hope Bob figures out how to speed up." "I
wonder when Bob will figure out how to work with this team
better." If you hear this in meetings or one-on-one conversations, do not brush it off. If you ignore it, the fire will become
bigger. Don't get defensive, but ask probing questions like, "Oh,
can you tell me more?" If you have an individual development
plan for Bob on file, you will know all the projects he is working
on, how he is doing against his goals, and how his team feels
about him. If Bob is truly having issues, then let the feedback
giver know that you know what is going on and are actively
coaching Bob. Otherwise, you should dig in for more information. Try to fish for tangible instances of poor performance and
how to gather further feedback from multiple people. If the person comes up with real examples, it might indicate the start of
Bob's slide down into poor performance. In that case, thank the

other person for the feedback and commit to talking more to Bob and coaching him as necessary.

If the provocateur cannot provide any real examples or come up with others who can back up this feedback, then the critic is either gossiping or lying. In those cases, you have to tell the detractor that you disagree with their assertion firmly, and if they need further clarification, they can go to your boss or HR, but don't discuss it with other people. After that, you should talk to your HR representative about the interaction, including letting them know what you think of Bob's performance. This is when provocateurs typically back off. After all, the standard office provocateur doesn't want to help anyone. Gossip is enough to keep them going.

You can use the same technique with your boss if they question Bob's performance. In addition to doing everything in the previous section, also offer to share Bob's development plan with them as further proof. Most bosses are satisfied with that, and they move on. However, there will be rare moments when your manager disagrees with you and really does think that Bob has a performance problem. Maybe they have a personal grudge against Bob? Maybe they want to lay him off under the guise of a performance problem? If you truly believe Bob is an asset, you should stand behind it. You have to tell your boss that you can't disagree and commit. There are only two outcomes. Your boss, impressed by your conviction, decides that you are right and moves on, or they decide to go over you and fire Bob anyway. If your boss does the latter, you need to move on from the company. The first outcome is the more common one, so don't be afraid to push back.

A QUICK RECAP

1. Regularly assess team performance and keep the bar high by benchmarking team performance against others.

2. Address critical comments about team members promptly, probing for tangible examples and providing coaching or corrective action as needed.

3. If necessary, push back against unjustified criticism from superiors, prioritizing support for team members.

4. Stand behind valued team members if questioned by higher-ups, offering evidence like development plans to support their performance.

CHAPTER 13

How to Deliver Bad News on Poor Investment Decisions

In a past life, I was a midlevel product development executive at a midsize software company. Because I was a software product development leader, I owned both the product (what) and engineering (how) decisions. After my first year there, I was given the funding to extend the footprint of the product area that I owned in a significant fashion. Because it was such a major investment, everyone who was important at the company was closely watching our progress, including the CEO. This CEO was a phenomenal CEO who had been with the company for a while and had remarkably accurate intuition into how customers used the product. Naturally, he had a lot to say when it came to designing the new product. My team, on the other hand, followed the research and customer feedback to figure out what to build. This was where the CEO started butting heads with my team. He disagreed with my team about how the product should work. After a couple of frustrating meetings with the CEO, my project lead basically gave up, came to me, and asked me to help resolve the situation.

I was terrified of the CEO. To be fair, I am terrified of most executives, but this CEO was a force of nature. Tall, built like a linebacker, a soul-piercing gaze, stubborn as an ox, extremely sharp, and well loved and respected by everyone. However, I also knew that he wasn't stubborn enough to ignore data. I gave myself a month to put together a document that explained, with data, why my team was right and the CEO was wrong. I spent the month collating all the data my team had collected over the past few months, including direct customer quotes, clips of customer interview videos, survey results, peer quotes, and so forth. Before I went to the CEO, I pressure-tested my document against the scrutiny of the CEO's lieutenants. I got a lot of great feedback, but I found that the executive team was almost evenly split in their preference about what the right thing to build was. I wasn't surprised that some folks on the executive team decided to side with the CEO even after reading the compelling evidence that my team had collected. Executive teams are extremely feudal in nature. Alliances are very important to the executives, and alignment with the CEO was the most important alliance to pay attention to.

However, the chief product officer, who was responsible for all product decisions, landed on my side, so I knew my team's decision was right. After incorporating all the feedback from the lieutenants, I sent the document to the CEO for a review. After a few nerve-racking weeks, I heard through the chief product officer that the CEO had greenlit the project as my team had envisioned. In the end, he couldn't ignore the evidence. My team went on to build that product, which turned out to be a hit with the customers.

Irrational Decisions

For a long time, I believed that corporate leaders would always make decisions that benefited their customers. That happy illusion was shattered in more than one way as I moved up the career ladder. The more time I spent with executives, middle managers, and board members, it became clear to me that, at the executive level, not all decisions are made looking through the lens of the customer, employees, or the broader business.

The executive space at the top often reminds me of the top of a very tall mountain where both space and oxygen are scarce. There is constant jostling among the executives for attention, budget, protecting territory, and personal ambition. Unless the CEO is a founder turned CEO, even their hold on the leadership seat is tenuous. All the executives at some level think they can do each other's jobs, including the CEO's.

All the pushing and pulling inside leadership teams sometimes leads to irrational decisions. When I say irrational decisions, I mean decisions that are made through the lens of the following:

- A decision an executive has committed to their board even though there is no data that proves the decision will be beneficial to the company

- A decision an executive has committed to the CEO even though there is no data to support it

- A project/feature an executive wants to push forward to curry favor with another executive as a quid pro quo

- A project/feature an executive wants to push forward (mostly to save face) even though there are flashing red signs that indicate the project will fail

Creative teams like product development, engineering, and design work best when they believe in the problem they are designing a solution for. The best creative teams will dig into the data (anecdotal and empirical) that supports the problem statement before they commit to solving it. If you force the team to work on a problem using the guise of disagree and commit, especially in scenarios where the data is not supporting the project, they will begrudgingly complete the project, but you will lose a tremendous amount of trust with the team. Disagree and commit only works when the data is unclear.

A case in point: Amazon's return-to-office mandate. Despite overwhelming evidence that showed an increase in productivity and personal happiness when people worked remotely, Amazon mandated that its employees return to their offices three days a week. Nearly thirty thousand employees signed a petition urging the CEO, Andy Jassy, to reverse that mandate.[17] In my

---

17 Eugene Kim, "Almost 30,000 Amazon Employees Have Signed an Internal Petition to Fight the Company's Return-to-Office Mandate: Read the Full Copy Here," *Business Insider*, March 10, 2023, https://www.businessinsider .com/amazon-return-to-office-policy-petition-30000-staff-remote-work -2023-3.

career, I haven't seen anything that galvanized Amazon employees like this mandate. The simple reasons behind this organized uproar were that (1) there was no evidence that supported this return-to-office mandate, and (2) Amazon expected its ultrasmart employees to disagree and commit to a dumb decision. The executives disagreed and committed to a dumb decision their CEO was making, but the broader team said nope. As a manager of people and a leader, you're expected by your team to push back and not disagree and commit in situations that warrant it.

The first step is to figure out if a project or initiative is big enough to take a potential "disagree and disagree some more" (DDSM) stance versus a disagree and commit. DDSM situations should be very rare. I think in all my career as a manager, I have only DDSM'd twice. An easy way to determine if a project/decision is big is to figure out if it's a one-way-door decision. One-way-door decisions are almost impossible to walk out of, and even when it is possible, it will be a very expensive endeavor for the company.

Here are some examples of one-way-door decisions:

1. A pricing or packaging change

2. An acquisition

3. Creating a new line of business (products, services, etc.)

4. Creating a nontrivial footprint (people and products) in a new geographical location

5. Changing the name of the company

6. Changing the company values

7. Changing the company's financial footprint/ownership dramatically (IPO, sale, SPAC, etc.)

8. Altering the infrastructure footprint dramatically, for example, going to bare metal from AWS/GCP or vice versa

9. Dramatically altering roles (e.g., removing certain job families) or compensation structures

10. Embarking on a new product/feature that is going to take more than twelve months and a full team (more than ten or so engineers, more than one product manager, and more than one designer)

Most managers typically encounter 10, 9, or 8, with 10 being the most common. If you are pushing back against anything besides 10, your chances of success are very low. The biggest reason being there is no immediate impact to the product or its customer base. Everything following this paragraph is going to focus on how to push back effectively—or how to deliver bad news—on a poor investment.

Disagreeing Strongly

Generally speaking, the approach to disagreeing strongly involves two phases. The first phase is to collect enough data that supports your point of view and following that up with enlisting other people on your team (peers, managers, engineers on your team, product managers, etc.) to pressure-test your theory. Most people fall into the dangerous trap of cherry-picking feedback that supports their theory. They seek out people who will support their point of view regardless of what the reality is. This path is extremely treacherous and will most likely end in defeat. Instead, actively seek out the contrarians, skeptics, and naysayers. Nobody likes to be proven wrong, but if you have decided to DDSM, you have to be absolutely sure your argument is rock solid. The strongest evidence you can gather is from your customers. To be clear, I am not suggesting asking your customers if your boss is an idiot or not. What I am suggesting is to start looking at any and all user research data, customer feedback, and so on to figure out if there is any evidence to support your stance.

Okay, so you have gathered enough evidence against a potentially bad decision your boss or your company is about to make. The next step is to write your counter proposal into a careful narrative that clearly describes your thought process, how you collected the data, who you got feedback from, and what your counter proposal is. Share it with your bosses for a pre-read, and pull them into a live meeting to discuss it further. In all likelihood, the minute your bosses (or whomever you are disagreeing with) get your written proposal they are going to start socializing it within their circles to get feedback about it. This is exactly what you want. Because you have already done your homework, you already know how most people will react to it. There is nothing better than making the universe work for you.

Even after all this, there is no guarantee that you will get your way. Executives and CEOs are used to making unpopular decisions, and they might end up ignoring your proposal anyway, but the important thing is you spoke your mind.

A QUICK RECAP

1. Push back on one-way-door decisions versus two-way-door decisions.

2. Effective pushback involves gathering data, listening to diverse perspectives, and presenting clear proposals.

3. Seek feedback from skeptics and customers for robust arguments.

4. Despite efforts, executives may proceed with unpopular decisions.

5. Becoming an effective manager involves speaking up and expressing dissent, regardless of outcome.

CHAPTER 14

How to Receive Bad News

A long time ago (or maybe a couple of months ago), I ran engineering for a small-size company headquartered west of the Mississippi. I was six months into the role, and I had made a great deal of positive changes in the organization, or at least I thought I did. I had managed out a handful of under-performing (or misaligned) leaders and individual contributors and replaced them with folks who had experience and/or the desire to operate in a high-performing meritocracy. To preserve a high talent bar, I also instituted a rigorous talent review process where, every month, I would meet with my leaders to figure out who was performing well and ready for a promotion, who wasn't working well and needed coaching, and who was beyond help and needed to be managed out of the company. At my six-month mark, the team was a good mix of old guard versus new guard. Anecdotal evidence showed that employees embraced the changes and loved the new direction in which we were headed. My leadership team loved my working style and loved working with me. My peer executives thought I was a great guy to work with. My boss decided that I was an okay executive to keep around. I thought things were going great, and I was floating at the top of the world. And then I was publicly shamed.

On a sunny morning, I got a Slack message from my boss with this message: "Did you read the latest Glassdoor review about engineering culture?? This isn't good!"

The two question marks and the exclamation point were a sure sign that it was serious. One of the bellwethers of culture at my company was its Glassdoor ratings. For the uninitiated, Glassdoor is a website where current and past employees can anonymously post reviews about their companies and give them a score. Scores range from one to five, with five being the best. If you look at any desirable employer, chances are their Glassdoor ratings are above four. My company was very proud of its Glassdoor ratings, and the respective department leaders scrutinized every poor review.

After my boss Slacked me, I frantically went to Glassdoor and started skimming through the latest reviews. The newest one sank my heart. I always knew that when I started making changes, some people might not like it, but I tried my best to keep the engineering culture from deteriorating. Instituting a meritocracy wasn't the only thing I did. I raised the salaries for about 80 percent of my team (one engineer's salary went up by $90,000 in two years) because I found out they were underpaid. I gave the high performers significant end-of-the-year bonuses and pushed to give employees an ownership stake in the company. I spent a good amount of time with all the teams to ensure their voice was heard and many other things, so the culture didn't go by the wayside. All of this was validated by consistent high-engagement scores in regular surveys the HR team ran. So, when I saw this stinker of a review, my heart sank.

Essentially, this anonymous employee accused me of "destroying the engineering culture," "pushing new agendas without fully understanding the implications," and "hiring cronies" to sow division inside the engineering organization with the ulterior motive of pushing the old guard out.

I am a fairly calm person and don't get riled up that quickly, but as I was staring at the Glassdoor review, my entire body seemed to heat up with rage. I was pressing my lips together so hard that it hurt my teeth. I was fairly upset with my boss. How dare he insinuate that something was wrong in my department. I knew my team better than anyone else, and I knew things were better than ever! At that moment, I wanted to yell at my boss for not understanding how hard it was to turn the ship around without breaking it in two. I wanted to reply back to my boss's Slack message saying, "You don't understand how hard it is!" and follow it up with, "I am going to find whoever wrote this and fire them today." All kinds of nasty emotions raged through my mind.

Then I remembered something important. The person raging was not me. I am not the leader who yells at his team or his boss. I am the one who calms them down when they are stressed. I am not a leader who shies away from accepting critical feedback, no matter how harsh it is. My boss was asking me to look into it because they cared about the company's culture and wanted to ensure the department leaders did the right thing. There was no malicious intent behind it. I was thinking about doing awful things that I coached people *not* to do. I took a deep breath, canceled my next meeting, and went for a walk around the building with a colleague. By the time my walk was done, my brain had successfully flushed out the negative thoughts, and I started feeling more like myself. I sat down and came up with a plan.

The fact of the matter was that it was one review, one data point. Hardly enough data to signal a trend. However, it still meant someone was unhappy with my changes. I replied back to my boss that I would look into the issue and get back to them. The next day, I brought up the negative review with my leadership team in my staff meeting. I explicitly told them not to go looking for who wrote it, but I encouraged them to talk to their team about the changes in engineering and how they felt about it. I also gently prodded my team when I talked to them. I cleared out my Friday afternoons to talk to whoever wanted to spend time with me. Ultimately, I wanted to encourage people to come to me directly with their concerns instead of anonymously raging on a public website. After mobilizing my leadership team, I got on a call with my boss and walked them through my approach. My boss was happy that I was taking this seriously and was satisfied with my approach.

After about three months, some of the individual contributors started reaching out to me directly. Some had feedback about the changes I was making, others had concerns, and, in general, everyone appreciated the fact that I was easily accessible to them. Ultimately, I achieved what I wanted to do: pull my team closer to me. I still get the occasional lashing on Glassdoor, but I know how to deal with it correctly.

The Aggravating Message

I am sure a lot of you have received the email, Slack message, text, or voicemail that leaves you completely harried after. The message that you can barely get through without cursing. Your hands become claws clutching your phone, wanting to shatter the gorilla glass, your brows are all scrunched up in impotent anger, and your lips are pressed so hard against each other that your teeth start to hurt a bit. Yes, it's a message from your boss indirectly (or sometimes directly) questioning your capabilities. You know, messages like these:

"I asked for this two weeks ago; how many times do you want me to repeat it?"

"I asked you to do it like this; why didn't you listen to me?"

"These timelines don't work for me."

"It's clear that Bob is not performing; what are you doing about it?"

"Why are you not doing anything about it?"

The more you read the message, the more your rage builds, and at some point, you are infuriated enough to want to punch a hole in the wall. Father Time comes to help apply a salve to your exasperation. Your rage subsides to a dull throb, but your day is now utterly ruined. Doubly ruined if it is a weekend. You walk around angry at everything and pull a dark, ominous cloud crackling with negative energy over your head for the rest of the day, which will zap anyone who comes close to it.

I have spent a lot of my brain cycles analyzing the phenomenon of "the Aggravating Message," both my own reactions to those messages and how to respond, and the writer's motivations, with the writer being, in most cases, the boss. This chapter is about this very common downer every manager has to deal with from time to time.

The Heat

The first thing to do is pause. There is no need to reply that instant. If your boss really wanted an immediate response, they would have called you. I can almost guarantee that if you decide to reply to it in the moment, you will send something that you will regret later. Anger and frustration grow exponentially when you feed them.

Take a deep breath, put your phone down, and go for a quick walk. If you can walk outside, even better. I can assure you that your boss doesn't want an immediate response, or, in some cases, they probably don't want a response at all. Your immediate goal should be to get your heart rate down to what it was before you read that message. Unclench your fist.

After you get your heart rate back to normal, go about your day for the next few hours if it is a workday, or longer if it is a weekend. By then, your prefrontal cortex (the rational part of your brain) should have taken over and you are now ready to tackle your response. I usually start by rubber ducking with a friend, peer, or mentor before I reply to anything. This usually allows me to get past my blind spots or any other residual anger from the first message.

One of the biggest epiphanies I have had after responding to thousands of angry work messages over the years is that often the emotional tone is lost in short-form text-based communication like Slack and texts. There is a distinct possibility that the sender didn't even intend to make you feel bad with an aggressive or passive-aggressive text message. This is another reason not to respond to the text message in the heat of the moment.

Okay, now your heart rate has come down, you have talked to a few people about how to respond to the message, and you have mentally prepared yourself to craft a response.

The Response

The very first thing I do is establish if there is a real ask in the message. For example, take this message: "These timelines don't work for me."

There is a distinct ask here. Your boss wants to know if the timelines can be pulled in, so your response should highlight why the project got delayed, what the team is doing about it, and what additional leadership help (resources, scope) can pull in the timelines.

Contrast that message with this one: "I asked for this two weeks ago; how many times do you want me to repeat it?"

There is no real ask here. This is your boss taking out their frustrations on you.

My basic rule of thumb is, if there is no real ask from your manager, you will have to get on a call with them to hash things out. If there is a real ask, the only situations where responding in text is appropriate are execution-related questions like project delays. Anything else, like personnel issues, I recommend having that conversation live.

If you are responding to project delays, stick with the formula I offered previously. Explain the delay, what you have learned from it, what you are doing about it, and what additional help (resources, scope change, etc.) can enable your team to move faster.

When you write your response, keep all emotions out of it. Just state the facts, ask for help (if needed), and extend an invitation to discuss it live, that's it. If your boss is unhappy with the response, you will hear from them, but if the message was just a cheap shot to release their frustrations, you won't. In this situation, no news is good news. In your next one-on-one, don't forget to bring up your response to make sure your manager is good with your responses.

The Live Conversation

If there is a tangible non-project-related ask from your manager (e.g., "It's clear that Bob is not performing; what are you doing about it?"), or if there is no real ask from your manager (e.g., "I asked for this two weeks ago; how many times do you want me to repeat it?"), you have to get on a call with your manager to hash things out. Essentially anything that veers into a gray area that has a gray answer necessitates a live conversation.

The key to a successful live meeting after a scathing text message is time. Specifically, its passing. It doesn't matter how hotheaded a person is, if you give time a chance, it will smooth over most surface anger. I recommend letting at least half a day go by until asking for a live meeting.

Here is a neat psychological trick to remember before getting on the call. Humans love to go hunting for confirmation. If you start the conversation by acknowledging that your manager's issue is a real issue worth solving, you have a decent shot at walking away unscathed. If you start the conversation by questioning your boss's point of view, you won't get far.

I know this is counter to what all the management books scream at you. They want you to dive into conflict, stand for your point of view, disagree, and so on. I am not saying you shouldn't do all that. What I am saying is, if you *start* the conversation with a confirmation, you are inviting your manager to lean into the conversation versus becoming defensive.

In the live meeting, stay pleasant, stay empathetic, don't get defensive, and start by giving your manager the benefit of the doubt. Managers are expected to absorb a lot of crap, and the higher you go, the bigger the serving. I always assume my manager is as stressed as me, if not more. So, if I managed to do something that made them lash out, I start with the assumption that I did something wrong. There is a small chance that your manager is a sociopath who doesn't deserve your grace, but those are few and far between.

If you are pleasant, empathetic, and self-critical, that conversation will go great. In fact, *all* conversations will go great when you are egoless. Your goal in the meeting is to get your manager to share their true intentions. And to get to their true intentions, you have to ask probing questions but not show an ounce of defensiveness or rudeness.

For example, if your manager is concerned about the performance of an individual, begin by asking for evidence instead of trying to defend the employee. You can eventually get to that in a *future* conversation, but your goal in the first meeting is to dig for facts. Use the "five whys" technique to get to the real issue and find time for a follow-up conversation. This technique, developed by Toyota, asks why five times to attempt to get to the root cause (or close) to a problem. Once you have established the evidence your manager has, use the next meeting to either provide counter evidence or a plan to fix the specific issue your manager has raised. For specific steps, check out Chapter 12.

If your manager's concern is around something you are doing wrong (e.g., "I asked for this two weeks ago; how many times do you want me to repeat it?"), you have dropped the ball one too many times and now your manager is annoyed. If you were simply unaware that you were dropping the ball, apologize, promise to do better, and do better next time. However, if you were knowingly dropping the ball, like I do once in a while (or maybe often; you all will never know!), there is usually only one explanation. There are far more important things you are focusing on. At Amazon, this phrase was commonly used inside management circles: You will always have a thousand different things to do. Prioritize ten of those and do three.

In the live meeting, walk your manager through your priority list and ask for their help to knock one of those things off your plate to accommodate the thing you were dropping on the floor. Usually this is when your manager will back off or work with you to figure out who else can take it on or get that item done in some other way. The key to making this all work is being self-critical all the way. If you get defensive, it will never work.

It also might be the case that the real issue your manager is dealing with is hidden beneath the surface. As mentioned previously, being a manager can often be lonely. The higher you climb, the lonelier it becomes. It is not just loneliness; it is also the stress that increases as you ascend corporate America. It is like climbing Mount Everest without an oxygen mask or a guide, surrounded by an all-encompassing, lifeless landscape. Capitalism, yay!

I consider myself a fairly empathetic person. In all my work relationships, I try to connect with my peers and reports in a way that encourages them to share their true intentions with me. Often, the key to get your colleagues to become vulnerable with you is for you to start first. All my work relationships, including relationships with bosses, that have been tempered by mutual vulnerability have been the most successful. Most of the rest fall apart over time.

In instances where I have a really solid relationship with my manager, I can navigate the case of the scathing message fairly easily. I start off by accepting responsibility and a promise to do better, but my real goal is to get them to talk about the invisible hand that pulled the trigger that sent the scathing message. I ask them questions like "How are you doing?" or "How are you feeling?" or "What is top of mind for you?" and so on. The minute the true reason that caused their outburst comes out, consider you and your manager to be good.

However, keep in mind that creating a relationship based on empathy and vulnerability takes time and effort. And there might be instances where you are never able to create a relationship with your manager. I have been in those situations, and I hate to say it, but it never ended well.

A QUICK RECAP

1. Practice doing the "pause" when you get hit sideways by a scathing message from your manager.

2. Figure out if there is a real ask from your manager or not.

3. Project-related questions can be delivered via text; everything else requires a live conversation.

4. If you dropped the ball, fess up and ask your manager to help prioritize.

5. Try to get to the root of your manager's behavior by establishing a relationship based on empathy and vulnerability.

How to Determine If You Will Thrive as a Manager

O ver my two decades in the software industry, I have come to realize that most people stumble into leadership roles rather than deliberately plan a path to those roles. Much of it is attributable to the quickly changing nature of technology. One day, you are happily coding away; the next day, your manager leaves at the exact moment your company's business is taking off, your boss's boss does a battlefield promotion, and *boom*, you are it! I can almost guarantee that most manager promotions are battlefield promotions for pre-IPO companies. This appendix offers a quick self-evaluation that any aspiring manager can take to determine if they really want to be a manager or not. Note that the evaluation does not determine whether you will be successful as a manager. There are a lot of great managers who don't want to be in the role, and there are many terrible managers who have been in the role for decades. Think of this evaluation as a self-reflection that you can go through to determine if you want to be a manager. Obviously, the more honest you are, the more accurate the results will be. Remember, no one else is looking at the results besides yourself, so be as self-critical as possible.

Q1: Do you easily share credit?

A: Y/N

Q2: Do you easily forgive and forget?

A: Y/N

Q3: Do you like exploring adjacent disciplines? For example, if you are a software developer, do you feel comfortable doing some QA? If you are a product manager, do you feel comfortable doing some design?

A: Y/N

Q4: Does clarifying ambiguity energize you?

A: Y/N

Q5: Do you embrace production support / customer support when the need arises?

A: Y/N

Q6: Do you try hard to keep up with the pace of the industry but feel you are perpetually behind?

A: Y/N

Q7: Does it bother you when you have arguments with your team?

A: Y/N

Q8: Do you understand the key business metrics of the company/team you currently work for? If not, are you willing and interested to learn them quickly?

A: Y/N

Q9: When your team misses deadlines, do you feel bad?

A: Y/N

If you answered yes for most of these questions, a people manager path is probably something worth exploring. There is no guarantee that you will be successful in it, but the initial signs look promising. Let's unpack the questions and the ethos behind them a bit further.

Do You Easily Share Credit?

One of the things I coach new people managers to get comfortable with is giving and not getting praise. If you are addicted to the quick hits of dopamine that praise provides, then a people manager path is probably not for you. Plays that managers run are long games. It isn't like crafting a nicely written piece of code or a requirements document. Managers make moves that will show results in months and years, not hours and days. In the past, I have seen results show up after I left the company and moved on. Here is a simple thought exercise to prove my point: Who is more popular, Patrick Mahomes (quarterback) or Andy Reid (coach)? People managers do what they do because they derive satisfaction from their long-term positive impact on the company. They do it because they want their people to succeed and grow. They are motivated from within.

I am sure many of you reading this are thinking aloud, "Yeah, sure, I can do this." Trust me, it is not easy. A consistent piece of feedback I have gotten from newer people leaders is that they don't feel appreciated and they don't receive enough praise. You can't expect praise after executing each play. You get the praise after all your plays ladder up to something meaningful for your company. Players can be praised for the effort they put in, but not coaches. Coaches can only claim long-term wins.

Do You Easily Forgive and Forget?

People management is an emotional roller coaster. Peers, bosses, and employees will question your ability to lead consistently regardless of which company you work for. You will often have to fight for scope, budget, promotions for your people, and so on, which means you will be disagreeing with a lot of people. If you are the type of person who holds grudges and remembers the names and faces of everyone who has ever done any wrong to you knowingly or unknowingly, you are probably not a good fit for a people manager role. Many managers find this out after realizing that all the baggage they keep in their mind will one day cause an emotional cave-in, resulting in them lashing out and other nasty consequences. The best managers don't hold on to the baggage. They easily forgive, forget, and move on.

Do You Like Exploring Adjacent Disciplines?

We are moving into a world where people managers are expected to manage increasingly heterogeneous teams. For example, engineering managers manage teams with front-end, back-end, and site reliability engineers (SRE). Product leaders are already managing teams with product managers, designers, research analysts, and so on. So how do good people managers manage folks with various specialties and backgrounds?

With curiosity.

They are intensely curious about how things work. With curiosity comes knowledge, and with knowledge comes humility and respect. If you are curious about a specific discipline that you don't have training in, you ask questions instead of making assumptions and passing judgment. This is what great managers do. They develop empathy and respect for the function (and the person) they are not skilled in by learning about it as much as they can, and they operate through constraints, guardrails, and outcomes as opposed to directives. For example, suppose your SRE team wants to use Kubernetes and comes to you for your blessing, and you don't have a background in operations or systems engineering. You don't tell them yes or no; instead, give them guardrails, constraints, and outcomes to drive toward that will help them make their own decision, for example:

1. Does the organization know enough about this solution to ramp up on it quickly? If not, what is the cost?

2. Why do we believe this solution is better than others? What other solutions did the team look at?

3. Can the team deliver it in under three months?

4. Will this fit inside our budget of X?

Additionally, you learn as much as you can about Kubernetes from online, figure out success and failure stories from other companies, and help provide your team with perspectives they might be missing.

Does Clarifying Ambiguity Energize You?

I am sure this is another topic where most readers would go, "Ambiguity . . . pfft . . . I eat ambiguity for breakfast." As a people manager, you will find the project and road-map-related ambiguities to be more complex than what you are used to as an individual contributor (IC), primarily because of the increase of stakeholders in the mix. If you are an IC, at the most, you are dealing with a handful of stakeholders, and you can safely ignore most of them, but as a people manager, you will be dealing with bigger, more opinionated, and very powerful stakeholders who cannot be ignored. You have to hear everyone's voice, alleviate everyone's concerns, and convince the naysayers to disagree and commit. And for large initiatives where everyone wants to grab a piece of the pie for various reasons (territorial, glory, etc.), this process can and will get exhausting. Exhausting but rewarding if you are willing to play the long game.

Do You Embrace Production Support/ Customer Support When the Need Arises?

This applies to anyone aspiring to get into a leadership role. Are you willing to do what needs to be done? Are you willing to get on the phone with an angry customer and help them out? Creative folks tremendously struggle with this. They can connect instantly with other like-minded creative folks but not so much with the customers who are not expecting creativity but service. They want their products to work consistently. They do not care about the strain your servers are under. Will you be comfortable explaining why your system went down (to someone who doesn't understand distributed systems) and convincing them it won't happen again (when you know it's impossible for a distributed system to have a 100 percent uptime)?

Do You Try Hard to Keep Up with the Pace of the Industry but Feel You Are Perpetually Behind?

The tech world is a quickly evolving world with evolving workforces. In my time as a manager, I have managed boomers, Gen Xers, millennials, and Gen Zers. I have also seen the evolution of the tech world, mainframes, distributed systems, the cloud, the mobile revolution, the AI boom, the SAAS explosion, and so on. If you want to survive as a leader and a tech manager, you must always stay in learning mode. Learning not just about technology and product trends but also about workforce trends, pop culture, socioeconomic developments and nuances, and so forth. Managing a Gen X employee is way different than managing a Gen Z. In people management, especially in the tech world, it is never one-size-fits-all. Your core management philosophies might stay the same, but the playbook will vary from company to company. Contrast that with an IC role, where you just have to worry about half of the equation. If you are a product manager, you only have to worry about keeping up with product and customer trends. You can easily shake your fist at the young'uns and tell them to get off your lawn. You can't do that if you are a product leader managing product managers of various ages, ethnicities, and backgrounds. So, if you are comfortable staying in perpetual learning mode, a people manager role is for you.

Does It Bother You When You Have Arguments with Your Team?

This is another way of asking, "Do you avoid conflict?" This one doesn't need a ton of explanation, but in short, people managers deal with a sizable amount of conflict. Conflict with employees, peers, bosses, executives, customers, other departments, and so on. To be clear, I don't think anyone is born with an innate ability to navigate and resolve conflicts. It is a skill that can be learned. However, if you are considering exploring a management path, you have to walk into it with your eyes wide open when it comes to conflicts. You will be expected to embrace it, navigate it, and resolve it. See my core tenets from Chapter 1 for reference.

Do You Understand the Key Business Metrics of the Company/Team You Currently Work For?

Here is a thought exercise. For the projects you work on, do you care more about the craftsmanship and quality of your individual work than the overall impact on your company? Do you understand how the work you do translates to overall success for the company? Do you know the trends of the success metrics? The best managers can draw a clear line between projects their employees are working on and the success metrics of the company. Managers who fail to do that will be left with a team that cares more about the craftsmanship of their work than whether it contributes to the success of the company. To be fully transparent, not every team does this well, but teams and managers who figure this out will have a much easier time aligning their team's motivation to the company's success. Here is a story one of my old bosses told me about twenty years ago. My boss's manager, the department head, used to manage the trading systems for a large brokerage firm. The department head would pull a weekly report of all the trades and associated fees that went through his system, highlight in bold the dollar amounts that contributed to the company's revenue, and send it to the CEO. He never missed his bonus.

When Your Team Misses Deadlines, Do You Feel Bad?

I can feel the hackles of the readers going up as they read this question, which looks like a pointy-haired boss wrote it. Here is a thought exercise. If you are an IC reading this, think about the project retrospectives you have been a part of. Do you bring up missed deadlines? Do you nudge the team into pathways that will enable the team to deliver faster? If you are asking these questions right now or are wondering why nobody else in the team is asking these questions, a career in management might be the right move for you.

For good or bad, most companies are driven by return on investment. They exist to build products that the public will pay for at a price that is financially meaningful for the company's shareholders. Success in capitalism is determined by urgency, invention, ingenuity, the occasional sacrifice, and some luck. Newer managers often forget the rules of the game they have decided to play. If you want to become a successful manager, you have to show a track record of consistent, financially meaningful delivery of products and services through your team. And you can't be consistent if you are not constantly adapting to the evolving market conditions around you. You have to continuously raise the bar.

However, there is another way to look at this, which is not purely capitalistic in nature, and that is to continuously raise the bar to just become better as a team. Most teams stay together for a limited time, at the most two years. Why not make it the best team you have ever worked in? A team that can move fast, delivers value to the business, continuously becomes a better version of itself, and takes care of its people is a great team to be a part of. If the idea of continuously raising the bar for your team is appealing to you, a path in management is worth considering.

ABOUT THE AUTHOR

Photography by Lorin Backe

MAHESH GURUSWAMY is a seasoned product development executive who has been in the software development space for over twenty years and has managed teams of varying sizes for over a decade. He is currently the chief technology officer at Kickstarter. Before that, he was an executive running product development teams at Mosaic, Kajabi, and Smartsheet.

Mahesh caught the writing bug from his favorite author, Stephen King. He started out writing short stories and eventually discovered that long-form writing was a great medium to share information with product development teams. The essays he wrote over the last few years culminated in this book.

Mahesh is passionate about mentoring others, especially folks who are interested in becoming a people manager and newer managers who are just getting started. Anyone interested in a one-on-one coaching session with him can reach out to him at sensibleexec@gmail.com or connect with him on LinkedIn (https://www.linkedin.com/in/maheshguruswamy/).

Mahesh resides in Orange County with his wife, Krishma, and son, Vivaan. In his free time, you can find him either running on the trails around South Orange County or reading cosmic horror fiction.